The Total Light Process

Kentucky Voices

Miss America Kissed Caleb
Billy C. Clark

The Total Light Process: New & Selected Poems
James Baker Hall

Famous People I Have Known
Ed McClanahan

Buffalo Dance: The Journey of York
Frank X Walker

The Total Light Process

New + Selected Poems

明

JAMES BAKER HALL

THE UNIVERSITY PRESS OF KENTUCKY

Publication of this volume was made possible in part
by a grant from the National Endowment for the Humanities.

The University Press of Kentucky
Scholarly publisher for the Commonwealth,
serving Bellarmine University, Berea College, Centre College of Kentucky, Eastern Kentucky University, The Filson Historical Society, Georgetown College, Kentucky Historical Society, Kentucky State University, Morehead State University, Murray State University, Northern Kentucky University, Transylvania University, University of Kentucky, University of Louisville, and Western Kentucky University.

Editorial and Sales Offices: The University Press of Kentucky
663 South Limestone Street, Lexington, Kentucky 40508-4008
www.kentuckypress.com

08 07 06 05 04   5 4 3 2 1

Cover photograph by James Baker Hall

Acknowledgment is made in the following for permission to reprint copyrighted material, some of which appears in slightly different form: Selections from *Getting It On Up to the Brag* and *Fast Signing Mute* reprinted by permission of Larkspur Press and the author. "The Buffalo," "Moonlight," "With Deer," "Hawkbells," "Washing My Cup in the Last Light," "Yet to Be Named," "Kneeling," "*Ars Poetica*," "This Kiss," "Names," "A Second Place over the Mountain," "Getting Naked," "Love," "Her Fingertips," "Desire," "The Fox," "Absence," "Home from the Hospital," "Prayer for the New Year," "Brother Prayer," "The Owl," "Little Man," "Young Man Comes of Age in America," "Our Mother's Hand," "It Felt So Good but Many Times I Cried," "Final," "Emerging Shadows at Sunset," "For My Mother on My Birthday Many Years after Her Death," "Requiem," "God's Overture," and "The Mother on the Other Side of the World" are from *The Mother on the Other Side of the World* by James Baker Hall, published by Sarabande Books, Inc. © 1999 by James Baker Hall. Reprinted by permission of Sarabande Books and the author. Material is reprinted from sections One, Two, Three, and Four of *Praeder's Letters* by James Baker Hall, published by Sarabande Books, Inc. © 2002 by James Baker Hall. Reprinted by permission of Sarabande Books and the author.

Library of Congress Cataloging-in-Publication Data

Hall, James Baker, 1935-
The total light process : new and selected poems / James Baker Hall.
p. cm.
Includes index.
ISBN 0-8131-2337-2 (alk. paper) — ISBN 0-8131-9114-9 (pbk. : alk. paper)
I. Title.
PS3558.A3685T68 2004
811'.54—dc22   2004014312

This book is printed on acid-free recycled paper meeting the requirements of the American National Standard for Permanence in Paper for Printed Library Materials.

Manufactured in the United States of America.

Member of the Association of
American University Presses

Acknowledgments

I'd like to thank the editors of the following periodicals for their support: the *Hudson Review*, the *Sewanee Review*, the *Paris Review*, the *New Yorker*, the *American Poetry Review*, *Poetry Northwest*, the *Kenyon Review*, the *Antioch Review*, the *Denver Quarterly*, *Wind*, the *American Scholar*, *Poetry International*, *Poetry Australia*, *Plainsong*, the *Cincinnati Poetry Review*, *Field*, the *Chariton Review*, *Quarterly West*, *Ironwood*, the *New Orleans Review*, *Poetry*, *Ploughshares*, *Telescope*, the *Massachusetts Review*, the *American Voice*, *Poetry Now*, and the *New York Quarterly*. And special thanks to Michael Tarachow and his Pentagram Press.

It's been my great good fortune for a while now to have exceptionally professional and personable people publishing my books. Sarah Gorham and Jeffrey Skinner at Sarabande Books are more than a wayfaring poet could dare hope for, and whoever answers the phone in the office there—Nickole Brown, Kirby Gann, Kristina McGrath—enhances the good fortune. And the same thing is true at the University Press of Kentucky, under Steve Wrinn's energetic and ambitious new leadership. The series in which this book appears, to the delight of its author, was his idea, and a very good one, and he's got a staff to deliver. I trust implicitly the people in the office there and have grown fond of them. Special thanks to Richard Farkas for his design work on this book, and to David Cobb—for keeping the ducks all in a row. Thanks also to Leila Salisbury, Gena Henry, and Anne Dean Watkins for various kinds of help and good fellowship.

JBH

For Larry, Matthew, and Michael

And, as always, for Mary Ann

Contents

from *Getting It On Up to the Brag* (1975) and *Fast Signing Mute* (1992)

from *Her Name* (1981)

from *Stopping on the Edge to Wave* (1988)

from *The Mother on the Other Side of the World* (1999)

from *Praeder's Letters* (2002)

New Poems

from

Getting It On Up to the Brag (1975)

and

Fast Signing Mute (1992)

The Poet Finds an Ephemeral Home in a Truck Stop on the New Jersey Turnpike, ca. 1970

for Bob Holman

Just look out there in the lot, dozens
of trailer trucks, each of them—
covered with road dirt: monumental
cartes blanches is what they are!
I see myself out there zapped up
like a billboard painter writing poems
on the dirty sides of those trailers
with my finger. I write, Title:
Introduction to Transcendental Numbers:
Poem: The greatness of living in Dwarf, Ky.
is all the others who aren't! Love, Jimmy.

Just think of all the people who'll read that!
Abstract expressionism in the Chase Manhattan,
and now poetry, poetry! on M&M trucks—
America by God will make it yet!

Picture the Babcocks, all seven of them
in their relatively new station wagon
passing my introductory poem on the way
to Grandma's house in Wilkes-Barre, Pa.,
picture that will you!
                                        And picture
eighteen year old Wayne Willis and his girl
sitting close in his souped up GTO
with a license plate that reads LUV ONE
in Topeka, Kansas, he and his girl

pull up beside my big trucking poem
at a stop light in Topeka, Kansas . . .

Dozens and dozens of poems, each
with a specific destination unknown
to me, au courant! I'm so excited!
I love 'Sailing to Byzantium,' I really do,
but times have a-changed! Take art
out from behind the glass! No more
corrasable bond, no more agents
and editors and all that New York shit!

Straight to Topeka, Kansas, to Wayne Willis,
and old Wayne and his girl, pulling
up beside my big poem, they'll see
how the letters are all equally clear,
and he'll say to his girl, Gee whiz,
that poet who found the ephemeral home
in the truck stop on the Jersey Turnpike
licks his motherhunching finger
after every letter, he's eating
America's road dirt for us!
And his girl will say, For us
and for his motherhunching art too!
Your preoccupation with pure motives,
Wayne, is a drag.
                                        And when I hear that
I'll know that I've arrived!
A mixed-media extravaganza, not
just words but calligraphy, the letters
themselves calligraphic analogues
to the poem's experience; and theater too,
a moving stage cannily subverting the old
tight-ass audience / art object relationship!

And so I up quick with another poem, it says,
Boston Bruins # 1, But You Know That!

And it's so clear now that I know
what I'm doing, that I'm where it's at—
consecrating our daily experience
with my art—that my next says simply,

Wayne Willis in souped up GTO and
girl sitting close in Topeka, Kansas,
I love you!
                    And when they see that,
they say, Wow, did you see *that*?

Captain Kentucky

for Ed McClanahan

1 . Road House, Saturday Night, Momma Comes After Her Boy, The Burly Bikerider, In Rambler American

Nobody hear her toot except him.
He keep quiet, nobody know maybe.
But he up and slam down bottle,
shout, Go home goddamn you Momma!

He got sixteen inch biceps.
He got black leather jacket with buckles.
He got big black stomping boots.
He got tattoos.
                    Just shut up,
Burly Bikerider, and nobody know!

But she toot more, louder he shout.

Now why he do that, you reckon?

For all the boyscouts in the basements of Baptist churches.
For all the little league coaches and umpires.
For all the sheriffs in Florida.
For all the class presidents and parachutists.
For all the full dress Marine sergeants in post offices.
For all the poets and teachers and lonesome truckdrivers,
   coffee stops with magnetic dogs from the vending machine.
For all the drivers of souped-up GTO's named The Judge.
For all the pro football fans.
For all the Jewish doctors.
For all us who got our picture in the paper, for all us who didn't.

We file out, form double line
from road house to Rambler American,
raise cocks like sabers in ceremony,

and every time she toot, we salute,
and every time he shout, we salute.
And so there we are, in tapestry forever, all
us Saturday night road houses lined up across America,
wasting our substance in riotous living. . . .

2. Captain Kentucky Is a Bomb Scare in Palo Alto

In real life, Momma finally leave, and guess what—
the B. B. follow her right out of the parking lot
into eternity yelling, Goddamn you Momma!
But in poem here he return to bar and grow long hair,
get freaky glasses, go off to college, join SDS.
And Momma back home puts Pepsodent in the cookie box
to send her son the revolutionary, she buy back linens
for him and his chick at white sale, she demonstrate for peace.
And when he scream about being co-opted at every turn,
she understands, and lets him turn her on.

Now why she do that, you reckon?

For all the family albums with dates beneath the pictures.
For all the women reading much read magazines at the hairdressers.
For all the gossips and gardeners and lady golfers.
For all the girl darkroom technicians.
For all the fat women named Norma.
For all the secretaries named Mrs. Dubois.
For all the schoolteachers who take aspirin for arthritis.
For all the women who wear white socks to the supermarket.
For all those who took piano lessons, and all those who didn't.

So when she comes to see me
I paint over the graffiti in the john
but leave the American flag curtains,
and when she asks whether that's patriotic,
I say, well, Momma, either it is or it isn't!
I'm a man now, Momma, and I'm so happy!

Gurney Norman, Kentucky Coal Field Orphan, Is Gurney Stronger Than History, or What?

There he is in the lookout on top of the mountain!
Binoculars, books, a typewriter, and a tape recorder.
Surrounding him on the walls are envelopes,
thousands of envelopes, one for each day he's lived.
When he recollects he writes his recollection down
and puts it in its proper place. He might be
the only man alive who remembers that day in 1944
when Max Terhune and his talking dummy performed
in the ballpark in Pennington Gap, Virginia.
Gurney's frail father left early on a Greyhound
for the VA hospital, his belongings in a paper sack.
Gurney's mother, hiding behind doors, was unhinged.
His paranoid uncle kept him up at night with a gun.
His granny bought a souped-up Chevy with Grandad's
cataract money. Listen to them rocker arms, she'd say,
you can't trust nobody about nothing no more.
Gurney's brother died in pieces on a railroad track.
Betrayal, loneliness, and loss, church boarding schools
with faggot coaches, hemorrhages on the kitchen floor,
kinfolks fighting, failure, guilt, abandonment, madness,
kinfolks sick and helpless, deaths in institutions,
there were shootings, and finally the strip miners came,
poisoned the wells and tore the very mountains down.
And yet, returning from his Grandad's funeral,
Gurney brought a suitcase full of Moonpies,
had a Moonpie and Dr. Pepper party, then dropped acid
on blast off for Apollo 11 at six the next morning.
The trick, he says, is to live in the present,
not the past or the future. The trick, I believe,
is to live like Gurney, in all three!

He says that all is as good as it could be,
and when he says that, who am I to say it isn't true?
I think that Gurney is the three gay-eyed Chinamen
climbing the mountain in the great Yeats poem!
Praise Gurney, he's King of the Mountain!

The Mad Farmer Stands Up in Kentucky for What He Thinks Is Right

There he is, crawling stomach and elbows across the frozen field,
apples in his pockets, binoculars tucked in his coveralls.
The mad farmer is a writer, teacher, naturalist, and family man.
He rests in his trek and eats an apple, shakes his fist
at the weekend warriors practicing bombs on the countryside.
The mad farmer drives a Scout, wears galoshes and a cap
with ears that tie under his chin. He gets the headache
when he goes to town twice a week to teach. Cincinnati money
has bought the next farm for hundred foot riverfront lots.
The mad farmer is under attack also by friends and family,
for being a communist, a reactionary, a liberal, a revolutionary,
a patriot, a cop-out, and a dangerous influence on the youth.
He makes it finally to the knoll, and sure enough, there they are,
wood ducks on the slough! there are dozens of wood ducks
on the slough!

Saturday Night, College Town, South, Young Fellow, Not Much Style, Waits for Score, in Earmuffs

He not Black.
He no Maoist.
He no parachutist.
He no filmmaker.
He got no Porsche.

College town hard on
who momma make live in dorm
and take taxi after twelve,
commies and preverts.

But he trying: street corner cool,
hands deep in pockets,
smokes big cigar in earmuffs.

Here come tight chinoes and pointy-toed shoes!
Here come bell-bottoms and square-toed shoes!
Just what he think, you reckon?
Chicks take off muffs to kiss ear?
He got vocabulary cards in pocket, this fellow.
Real fancy town think him
Andy Warhol in dis-guise,
Strom Thurmond in dis-guise,
second convolution nouveau no-sucky sex dealer,
sodomist smoking away smell of sheep shit.
But not here:
this Boone Country.

This Wildcat Country.
Our coach win game
for boys in Vietnam.

Then score comes, score of game
from round mouth of girl comes,
and muff smile.
He suck big cigar and blow
both sides big smoky man smile,
for score of game good. He happy,
team win, he awful happy!
Beat meat in dorm room happy now!
Whole town happy! Horns toot,
coach hero, whole town
go home beat meat happy now!

The Modern Chinese History Professor Plays Pool Every Tuesday and Thursday after Dinner with His Favorite Student

There they are in the billiard room of the faculty club.
A Chinese boy in a white coat serves them brandy.
The Professor, distinguished in his late forties,
bent over the brilliant felt in the low light,
strokes his cue with passion for the game.
Across the table, in bell-bottoms and a floppy hat,
his student holds her cue with both hands like a standard.
She has a full sensual mouth, is writing on Mao in Hunan.
In the shadows against the wall, high kneed on a high chair,
sits the Professor's doughty wife in her overcoat. She grips
her purse and smiles, as though someone were watching.
She tries to follow the game, but doesn't know the rules.
The balls click in the basement billiard room of this girls'
  school,
while upstairs, comfortable and intricate in their learning,
the Professor's colleagues analyze all their sick friends—
discussing at the moment who's the saddest,
the Professor, or his wife, or the young lady.

The American Love Song of the Mean Mary Jean Machine

Strapped to the roof rack of her
silver mint Carrera: a surfboard
and a bobsled and boxes of live
pheasants and rabbits for her hawks.
It's the Mean Mary Jean Machine,
the green flag on pride, a one-lady
field guide to the Western birds.
She wears a crocheted white wool
cottage industry Guatemalan power
hat, and a cottage industry purple
cotton Guatemalan power shirt,
and her custom yellow shades are
perched on the power hat like
a Gold Eagle's eyes. On the seat
beside her, two Russian Wolf Hounds,
and in the back, in custom leather
tote bags, a black M-4 Leica,
a one eighty Blad, and a big mean
peregrine on its perch.
                                        Whoooeee!
Here she comes, shooting the California
mountain passes on her way to her song.
This lady's lyric is in the point spreads,
somewhere between a redtail on a bunny
and a goshawk on a jack. She's up
to her bumpers in leaf mold, and
getting it on up to the brag.
                                              At her
ten-dollar-a-head concert they sell
stickers that say DON'T SHOOT HAWKS
and THE MEAN MARY JEAN MACHINE—
                                                                  all
the money marked for Bangladesh.
She feeds more hungry people
than the church.

The Family of Man Resides in the House of Philosophy

When the six year old asks
the ten year old why he keeps
opening and closing the stove
on his grilled cheese sandwich,
the ten year old answers
by asking the six year old
why he keeps spreading butter
on his bread, and when they keep
asking one another those same
questions over and over, the parents
get into it, asking them over and over
why they keep asking one another
those same dumb questions—

                                                            and
it is decided finally that nobody
has the slightest idea why
he does anything—
                                        which seems
to make them all feel a lot
better, so they shut up
for a while, and eat.

Rough Ride

Four year old brown and grey Ford family car, dirty
windows, full of dilapidated
boxes and clothes, young woman,
long wind-blown blond hair,
enters the parking lot
through the exit, takes
at the wrong angle both
available spaces, slumps
forward and cuts
the motor

which runs on, coughs, knocks,
pings, shivers—

                    she grants it,
pausing at the mirror, one last
chance, then whacks the dashboard
with a comb

                  and nods approval
at the final sigh—

                      disappears,
reappears, checks the mirror
one last time, throws her shoulder
to the door and rolls

out: three hundred pounds
in new bright blue slacks,
one shiny white sandal on, the other

hooked by the heel strap on the little finger
of her left hand which she holds high up
in triumph, she laughs

displays her bare foot and ankle, laughing,
and wiggles her toes

At the slim younger man,
blond hair falling over one eye,
white tee-shirt hanging out,
who has pulled in behind her
in an old blue and white delivery truck
with no door, KASATOV in red, white and blue letters,
New England's Finest Bakery, big clunker,
dirty wheels and dents,

                                        and with a grin
descends from the driver's stool, new
tan hook-lace work shoes, blue
gabardine pants, hands
stuffed in pockets
                                  to watch, smiling
as she wiggles her naked foot and ankle, kicks
off the other sandal and
with mock anger throws
them both into the car.

They have a conference there
in the parking lot, 6:56 P.M.,
May, Connecticut evening, college town
after finals, families mostly
out for ice cream, pretending
not to notice.

                                  He gives her
a twenty dollar bill which she takes
thumb and forefinger by the corner—
all the while griping about her car—

and like a tenderfoot on gravel
heads off across the asphalt
for a hot fudge sundae, holding
the big bill like a hanky
for balance

                    while he stands there
next to his still-running
old truck trying
to out-gripe her

and watches sheepishly
(flicking a cigarette)
all that incredible flesh.

As they get farther apart
they brag more loudly,
who has the roughest ride.

Stuffing It

in the express lane carton of half & half bag
of coconut chocolate chip cookies 6:36 P.M.
of a wednesday
behind an old lady
who has taken you would not believe
how long already not to buy
a quart of milk a package of juicy fruit
and pall mall longs
every time
you think there's nothing left to do
but pay and leave she finds it

or more nearly they find one another
like the balance sheet in her checkbook
it came to her as a kind of slow motion
vision and she wandered in first this month
then last the way an infant enters
rapt attention when it discovers
something in its hand
she is balancing
her checkbook three months back now
okay
when what I want
is a cup of coffee half
medaglia d'oro half kroger
alone and quiet for a few minutes
before I go to work
I still think
I've got something better to do
than stand here waiting while she gets
the cashier so flustered he can no longer
find the pall mall longs gone all of them cases
because he wasn't even sure then but thought
he gave them to her a long time ago when
he wasn't sure but thought he rang up
her purchase

I can see it coming
she'll get two viceroys
what she really wants
anyway but has forgotten
and not have to pay for either
because nobody
can do anything with her we'd give her the store
to get her out of here a half dozen of us we've tried
another line is forming in front of her
behind the guy in front of me who tried
seeing what he hoped was the end
to volunteer the pennies
which got everybody so confused
he's out of line with people lining up
behind him trying not to explain
the pennies still lying on the counter
which he gave up explaining back there
when she was the only one in the store
who didn't know what they were for
hadn't even seen the damn things yet
but trying to apologize to her
for his existence

perhaps this is the form
the second coming is to assume
Dr. J dressed up in 75-year-old white-boss
drag taking the whole system
one-on-one to the hoop
and stuffing it

stuff it to us old lady crazy
stuff it to us grandma

she's into her address book now
mistaking it for her change purse

who else but god gets two of everything free
for causing a disaster who else but god

has everybody in the world solicitous
because she acts as though they don't exist

on the way finally
I pass her standing
at the magazine rack facing
the wrong way in a daze

and decide to eat a cookie instead

New Morning

for Tanya

The plane lifts again and banks
like a conductor's gesture
the windows become a prism
playing a bar of colorful notes
to the measure of Kansas down there
farm houses fields crossroads vehicles

and I imagine her listening to the news
as she does the dishes and the children
rushing from the bus onto the playground
and the man of the house pausing at the back
door as he gets a feel for the day's weather

and I see each happening within
a circle of all colors

it is no more or less
Kansas down there
than it is up here

Moment

for Joan

Through the skylight
above the tub
the sun
cracks suddenly
like a crisp nut
echoes off the porcelain
and off the water
and shatters onto the white walls
a dancing shell of light.

And there she is
revealed once again
in the center
her long tanned body
the fruit of this moment.

When she breathes
the light
on the walls breathes
with her.

Item One in a General Theory of Things

for Barry Spacks

I remember a scene from *The Sophomore*:
Harry Zissel happens to be across
the street from a big city phone company
at 5:30 when the operators & secretaries
get off.

All of a sudden the building
opens up and out pours a jackpot of women
in their summer dresses, 400–500 of them,
it's beautiful.

Sometimes I think the whole
world has turned into a phone company
at 5:30. Sometimes I can hardly remember
seeing a man for days.

What's happened
to all the men? If I thought the rest
of them would disappear, and leave me
here, it would be one thing, but I can't
think men don't amount to anything any more
without thinking less of myself.

I can't
walk to work anymore without falling
in love three or four times.

It's exhausting!
Where are all these women coming from?
I've got other things to do—

Grace Abounding to the Least of Sinners

It all ends with the fat lady
at ringside, having watched
intently for a long time
as the great men wrestle,
thumbing her nose
and walking out,
                    showing them
the rolls of her stockings
on the backs of her knees.

The Master at His Early Morning

> The blessed good stuff, sitting up, in its
> myriad forms. . . . The ideally handsome way is
> for me to multiply in any given connexion
> all sources of entertainment. . . . It all
> comes back to that, to my and your 'fun'—
> if we but allow the term its full extension.
> —Henry James

When the kettle whistles and I'm still in the outhouse
reading *The Golden Bowl* and Onion comes wagging her tail
through the dew two and a half steps up and sticks her nose
under the book, asking of the master what, ideally,
this bright morning, given all the connections,
he has to say
and I tell her—

her tongue so to speak
understands, her cold nose
in my hand—fun.
We give ourselves
full extension,
the blessed good stuff,
sitting up, in its forms—

the dew steams in the low light,
a jay down the hill pumps
his handle, the new red
canvas of the lawn chair

has its handsome way
against the low grey fieldstone fence
where the cat now walks, a bright outline
of connections. It all comes back,

as the early morning
but allows, to this—

my tongue curling up
from the warm coffee
I will cup soon
in my cold hands,
a lighted cigarette
in the blue tray, the sun
behind it—the mere thought

multiplying through the light
like vapors, whistling, brightly,
its myriad forms.

from

Her Name (1981)

you remember
how many things come to one name
hoping to be fed

it changes but the name for it
is still the same
I tell you it is still the same

—W. S. Merwin

WHERE WE WAIT

If the heaviest creature
capable of flight weighs
forty pounds, only
on the moon will we be
light enough to fly.

We have always known that
for like any creature
heavy with death we are
forever trying
to forget—
                        as witness
our dreams: when at the moment
of flight we try to rouse
the loved one to go
with us.

                It is frightening
what she does to me,
waxing & waning
as though I do not
exist.

              There is a side
to the moon that never
shows, but we know
that it's there,
like grace,
in the old dreams
of falling

Hands

Whenever he leaves
for his constitutional, she
asks him to bring back a roll
of Tums, dozens of rolls

all over the house, many
of them not even started. She

is working a jigsaw puzzle
on the dining room table, her hands
beneath a gooseneck lamp move
in & out of the light. He

does not tell her she has turned
all the pieces backside up, she

thinks his eyes are too old
to care.

                    A pretty picture
on the box top is propped up
for both to pretend
to see.

                    When he falls
asleep, she puts one hand
over his, shifts

the grandchild
in her lap

& continues

At the Grave

Bricks hang from limbs
in the cemetery, training
them to grow down. Grackles
feed in the grass.

                    On an ornate
wrought iron bench painted white
two children, he
in a dark sweatshirt leans
over the back, head
gone, she
sits pensively, chin in small
hands. In the distance

the sound of mallards
and of one metal wheel
rolling over sandy concrete.

At night the darkness performs
for the eye, a silence broken
here by lightning, there
by small fires

Her Hand

Lying on the wood floor
next to the bed
like an orange peel, curled,
white, stringy

I can imagine
too what she saw: her frail blond son
of eight standing in the doorway
wearing coveralls to protect
his skin

One last
torment before she waved
it all away

I see her there
often, sprawled on the bed
with one arm flung
over the side, the hand
lying palm up on the floor
next to the gun

Her white gown is like
a blotter, blood blooms all
over her heaving red chest, she
goes down, her eyes
go down

I was playing
on a step ladder in the yard,
the handyman was pruning trees.
I heard the shot too, but

did not know it until he said
Oh my god! Miss Lurline! Miss Lurline!
I was afraid to follow him, afraid
to be left alone

Something Between Them

At first they appear
to be merely standing
there, a young Hispanic
girl, fat, half-
hidden in the ratty grape-
vine overgrowing the chain-
link fence, three grocery carts
in the project parking lot, two
overturned, Puerto Ricans & Blacks
just out of school, hot, no nets
on the baskets, hydrant flooding
the street. She

seems only incidentally
related to the older
male
        standing on the edge
of the sidewalk, very exactly
not looking at her, hair short, thin
moustache, also Hispanic, fancy
sports shirt with sleeves
rolled, thin
arms, cheap
bluejeans too big
                                        But
there is something between
them: he is
as close to her
as being seen
permits, she
as far away
as she dares
to get—

                At the corner
two teenage girls, bare

midriffs, tight pants, bare
arms & shoulder
bags cocked up

are hitch-
hiking

AT WORK

they never spoke, but
she knew who was calling

the minute she heard the breathing,
not a word, just breathing

the sound of another woman
breathing—

                    She taps the pack
of cigarettes to the edge of the dresser,
tips it with a pencil so that one
will fall

               (outside
her drunken boss is
tossing pennies
at the bedroom window)

Takes the phone into the closet
where it's dark

/

                         On the way
home from work, whenever
the traffic is bad, she

slips out of her underpants
into the middle lane
& turns off the radio
to concentrate

Bumper to bumper
doorhandle to doorhandle

her hand between her legs
she feels men sometimes
watching her

Stares
straight ahead, hardly
even smiling

/

First the tip
of the index finger
of the left hand

as though a string
were tied tight

She keeps trying
to remember whatever it is she is
supposed to
remember, it is storming

in the mountains. When she gets home
a letter will be
there, & then soon
a long distance
call. She imagines

an accident, the phone ringing all
night in her empty
house

Then a whole finger
on the other hand, all signs

say move left, move right
road narrows

She is gripping
the wheel too tight

In the Exit Lane

Dragging a scrap
of tire through a puddle
a wet bitch knuckles under
her shoulder blades, a scrawny fist
of eyes like yours, dares
everything in sight. Look

it is not my fault it rained today.
It is not even your mother's fault.
Take whatever you can
in your teeth, drag it
wherever you are going.
It is a long way.

I want off here.

This Is a Love Poem to You

for Susan

November 18, our code
for surrender, once
to love, now to disorder
& sorrow. I am no longer

in love with love, no longer
in love with life. If I love

it is you
I love, your voice,
your arms, legs,
neck, hands, your long flat wrists
where particular bracelets turn
with each day's weather,
each night's. If I love

it is as the weather gathers
& turns in the mountains where you are,
as the bracelets turn & gather
your skins, as the weather turns
& gathers me here where I am

alone. What we mean now
by desire is not simple.
What we mean now by desire
is beyond me. What we mean
is like ourselves,
whatever is obvious
& will not vanish—

From Where I Am Now

I am watching a grackle walk
around on a green lawn,
his bright yellow eye

a black period
at the center, no bigger
than a hole

on the horizon. I fall
into orbit around
the bright yellow eye

of a bird, common enough
between bodies, it is
like this

this life. I feel myself
being drawn in, I feel
myself being
stretched, I feel
my chest collapsing

Where is she? I see
her face, I hear
her voice, I feel
her lips opening

my eyes

2/ You see nothing
The heart itself would be

no bigger than a hole

many miles away A hole
many years away Her

absence in everything
All that is obvious
but unverifiable
The inferences

of gravity Tight spots
are followed by tighter
The heart flies

into itself
like a bird
Whatever is

obviously beyond us
can be known only
by what it does
to known things
The familiar effect

of bodies Tides
of attraction Tides
of release The look

on her face
I keep coming back
to the blood
that sees me The look
on my dying mother's face

3/ From where I am now
a half acre of terrace falls
gently from the screen porch

down to the steps, the steps
down to the rocky shore

a close-cropped bright green
foreground. Above it
a strip of water,
shades of grey-blue, flat, no wind. Light floats

on the surface
like a spill. Above that
the empty sky   Birds

their flight a beautiful
script writes them down
to the lawn

                              One
after another they swoop
down, hang like commas
above the grass

then drop abruptly
onto their shadows, period

You are wherever you are,
I am however I am,
the birds are on a Cape Ann lawn
12 :17 p.m. 20 June 1977, so to speak,
a metaphor of themselves

& all things
that die

                    The sun
sinks to a copper
on the horizon, placed

on my lidded eyes

The Cloudless Sky Takes Charge

The place to see
lightning is the desert, the sky
behind it, all around it

Like a great lizard
flicking out its tongue

The egg of darkness cracked,
a brief glimpse
at the other side

We lie there
face to face
back to back

caught in the shadows
on the wall

2 / The natural inclination
is down, except
for fire

In worship
the eye drifts upward
like a soul
to the sky

where it sees nothing
The most eventless of ordinary
skies, grey expanse, a huge
emptiness horizon to horizon

like a word repeated until
the meaning is gone, sky

after grey sky:
nothing in it

3 / Her eyes
deal these days
with fire, gathering

first this, then
that, the kindling

of all her illusions, finally
even love itself. I watch

her recede
into the one gaze
burning all. And what

I ask is the purpose of this
And she answers
with fire

4 / Like stars, collapsing
in on ourselves

if that is our fate
then we can be like stars

In the end nothing is left
but core, so dense

collisions are no longer
important, heat no longer
involved

5 / The cloudless sky takes charge
from the earth, charge after charge
goes up, clouds form

to gather it
& to send it back

flowering thru the empty places, lightning
in two forms, of the daughter by the mother
of darkness, as fire
& as higher light

We always picture lightning within a cloud
or cloud to cloud, or cloud to air
or cloud to ground, never

ground to cloud

But there it is, here it is
At the center a woman tends
& guards the fire

Only change is at work here
in the night sky, only
the goddess of opposites

is whole

During the Night

one of the seven sleepers
was taken by a slow, fluid elongation
of his features head first

through a hole in the wall
several feet above his pallet.

Like a forked tongue drawn back
into the maw. There was no
sound. This shows

that six men slept
through an entire night
in which their lives
were understood finally

as a dream. Toward dawn
the argument ensued

concerning the extent
to which his features
were distorted at the moment

of disappearance & the meaning
of that aspect of the event. This shows
that what lay inside the hole
was known to all.
They fully expected
to meet wickedness on the road
outside, shaped
as a man. They even believed

they would recognize him
as their lost friend

& with his wine sack
welcome him back.

This shows how the Mother draws,
up thc flue of darkness.
What voice is this

trailing him like soot, wafting him
into the night like smoke?
In the circulation

of early light she appears
young. Having risen from a lover's sleep
she makes her way
with a clothes basket

to the river

from

Stopping on the Edge to Wave (1988)

Sitting Between Two Mirrors

What I like best
is making lists of what I like
best. The good days

are inventories, near and far. I seldom leave
without a book. Where would I go without a book?
You would say my life is a lottery—
that I am the only one

without a ticket. You would say
your life is better—you say it over and over,
you do. What do I do? I put things in boxes.

I move boxes around. I have many things,
some of them mine. I care for them.
That is what I do. I do simple things.
I move them around, clearing places
to move them around. I tell you
I do things, over and over.
Now you tell me

something. Talk is what you do. It comforts
me to hear you talk. You would say that you are
mine too, my not-simple thing. Say it
again, today, I want to hear you say
something, today. I wash your clothes.
I buy you fresh bread.
I get the paper

to see what day it is. I laugh. I act
as though I know what day it is. I laugh
again—it comforts me to hear you
laugh. I talk

on the phone. I water the plants while I talk
on the phone. I make coffee while I talk
on the phone. I am a person
like anyone else. I act
like a person. A person

calls and says whatever it is
a person says. Says
today. A person says today.
I say today

over and over, getting it straight. Getting it
straight is what I do, I want to get it
straight. I say

What did you say?
Tell me something again,
comfort me.
Today? Yes, today.
Is that it?
And when is that?

To Get There

There is no place to go,
it takes a long time
to get there. At eleven-twenty each night

the mounted police come out
of a gold light in one window, two abreast,
and disappear into it

through another, the sound
of hooves on pavement, many of them.
It goes away, slowly, opening
the place up

and out. I am watching
the buildings become buildings
again. They empty into the streets,
the streets into cabs, the streets
are full of empty cabs—always
going somewhere—

Reading Palms

for Margaret Gibson

Legless and blind he sits in the middle of the
sidewalk on a newspaper,
head down, hand raised, shaking
the emptiness of his palm.
At times I can almost hear

our hands take shape above his, opening
and closing. Can feel him feeling the light
fall, the rain turning to snow,
the blind coins falling,
great distances,
into his palm.
Where is he,

I've always wondered, when he is not here?
How does he get there? How long
would it take me to see him move?

Organdy Curtains, Window, South Bank of the Ohio

I lived the whole time with my hands cupped to the
 open eye,
the light advancing like a flock of turkeys.
If the shadow of the catalpa touched

the sun wall of the house at 3:30
I waited several minutes
and entered behind it,
branching out slowly,

respectful of such a broad expanse of white, of silence,
the one small window, a mother's hand, that once,
at the curtain. I knew when to look head on,
when to squint. Things happened, beginning with her,

the way things happen on a clothesline, flashes
of this or that against the sky,
colors, faces, lips moving, snatches of faces—

Then suddenly no wind at all. Light hangs in the organdy,
south bank of the Ohio, I don't remember the year.
I can tell by the way my protective hands move
which eye is open, how vast the orphanage
of silence, how still
each blade of tall grass.
Once inside I am alone

briefly, hanging there,
in the light.

That First Kite

in memory of Ralph Eugene Meatyard

That first kite was made of newspaper and strung
with fish line. I was lying next to it, alone. Sunlight
in the bright shape of a window, X-ed once
with the shadow of the sash, moved

slowly across the floor toward
me. A way had to be found

to make it work. We were trying. All this
took place in the attic where the cat brought
the birds.
                              My mother was downstairs
or out back in the cornfield
with a gun.
                                   I didn't movc. Who knew
where my father was.
Nothing ever worked.
I kept my eyes closed

whenever I thought
I was asleep
or flying. I awoke

when I felt the light touch
my feet, perfect, still

I didn't move. When it touched
my eyes I opened. The crosshairs
were on my chest, breathing. I saw
my heart. A cold wind rattled
the kite.

Throwing Rocks into the River

Even when I was asleep in them the big beds
  seemed unused.
The tufted spreads, each fold perfect, light
the only other thing in the room. My eyes

indistinguishable from the white patterns
at first, and weightless—then

blue, splashing, the pupils collapsing inward. Sometimes
my feet were too small,
much too far away,
the light

had to work hard to reach me.
I repeated certain words until the meaning was gone, death
my favorite, then stood in front of a mirror and kept
  moving.
At an aunt's house, or a friend's, even at home, always

one step ahead
I disappeared
into the folds

(silence, then maybe a sound
as I went under, light
kicking up. Then
silence again. My mother first,
then soon my grandfather—already

I couldn't remember anything, twice).
One step ahead of what,
of what—oh, that's the question! Every time it's
  asked of me
I weigh myself for answer. A hotel room somewhere,

the low window, organdy, a breeze,
the curving wall with the mirror

backing light—
And across the street

at the train station
a solitary man
picking up rocks
from the track bed

throwing them into the river—

The Maps

All those years he was married,
frequenting the map stores.
The eight quadrangles surrounding the house
in which he lived and worked, he saw them in relief;
he pinned them over his desk like messages, justified.
He spent long hours studying them. He fell in love

with maps. At night he would lie on the couch
with his hands, in the dark, memorizing
the mountains. He would lie
on the floor in his son's room,
in the moonlight, the maps
between them. His hands
loved the waters, an island
at a time. His voice loved
distances. At some point
he quit, I quit

calling myself he.
I fell in love without maps.
I carried everything I thought I needed
in the back of a truck or in a knapsack,
I spent night after night lost in the darkness,
huddled on a beach somewhere, or asleep
on a stranger's floor. It took years.
I had to go all the way

to the white undersides of the leaves
before I knew when my own veins were shaking,
in the dog's ears, in the wind,

and it could occur to me, more often now,
that I need nothing. That I can, even yet,
quit calling myself anything.

Freeing the Sparks

I watch from the foot of the bed.
It rises at the end of what we can see

of 9th Street, a fireball in the alley
of tall buildings, exploding
in great pins of light.
I forget to think.
I forget everything
I have thought. Light is

what's left, alleging
to have forgotten nothing.
The brown walls, the peeling paint,
first one mirror
and then another.
My hand is here

standing on its fingers.
Each day a place stands up within
the light itself, the pulses open—
We call it

here—the brown walls,
the books, the red blanket, the plants
under the east-facing window

The First Winter Light

for Barry Spacks

The first winter light means
that I am standing still
long enough again to see it.
It comes around the corner, across the floor,
a band of it kneels over the stove and up
the wall. It offers colors
from the other room. My hand is

in the sun, pouring water
from the kettle—winter light
in the steam, in the blue fire.
On the edge

of the bright band,
off the bevel of the mirror,
a narrow rainbow is wrapped around
the shape of the stove, like a ribbon.
It comes in from the other room

and crosses the floor, it mounts the stove
as though it knows it perfectly, from the beginning
has been witnessing its shape, now
is the time—

the rainbow runs flat between the burners
and mounts the back of the stove.
It steps up the shelves
on the wall. I forget
that I am afraid
and then remember again

that someday I will see all this for the last time.
The light is in the spices, it is lined up on the wall.
It is in the pink grapefruit, halved,
on the stove. The sunlight has in it
the deep reds and browns
of the other room.
At any time now

I will go into the other room. I will turn
on the standing lamp next to the big chair.
I will smooth out the red blanket and sit down.
I will put the blue cup, steaming, on the corner
of the table, a few inches from my hand.
Until it happens

I stand here watching the colors.

Identifying the Body

I see that his brown eyes are open, ecstatic.
I see the thin shaft of his body.

We know that he did not sleep or eat for seven days,
that for months he was elsewhere, a whole world
of less and less;
that he rode the elevator up sixteen floors
at the Court House on Centre Street in Manhattan,
finding there, at twenty,
a place of justice.
He knew

that he or the world one was inverted.
His fast, we can imagine, was a weight
in his body, the higher he took it
the heavier it got. Through
a tall window

he slid, hung
his ankle to nothing. Gravity
in his brown hair, in his eyes, open,
in his smile. We offer such prayers
as we know.

The handbills in his backpack found
on the window ledge call for peace.
I see the Brooklyn Bridge as he saw it,
then Columbus Park where three boys play ball,
then the rush of windows, rising. In one

a chance witness

reaches out.

The Wedding Rings

In the Garden of Children

Gathered in the background, in the flickering
shadows of the fire, the fathers have no sound
for their grief, even their faces
are clear

smudges in the dark. On the dark terraces behind
them, in chorus,
the silent mothers

expand, the night sky wheeling.
The earth rolls over, night
after night, I turn

the corners, on foot
or in a car, the ecliptic vaulting
out of the shape of a particular
tree, suddenly there

they are, always
one child in the middle, ablaze, an airy form
ignited, her bright visage at the center of the fire or
it's a boy, his eyes closed, or
more than one child, burning.
It is not clear who

did this or why. No one
rushes forth to save them.
None of the children cries.
The parents bear witness.
There is no sound.

Main Case

An old house, the roof
buckled, the windows gone, the porch
on its knees. Harsh
midsummer sun, the weeds full of insects,
they fly up. The air is dry
and dusty. The weeds
advance

through the blinding sun and change
when they enter the shadow
of the house. Or take the light
into a different place. A woman,
there, one arm extended
over her head, one hand
in the sunlight,
pulls

a branch of the dead tree
like a bell rope, in and then out
of the light. She appears to be

waving. It is her smile—
a long preface

to the assembly of the broken house,
the weeds, the light, this ringing

of her body ringing
mine. In the main case
which we approach

a man watches a woman
play with him
in the shadows.

Seventeen-Year Locust

We wedge the bar into the cracks, prying flat stones
from the path of the old burned-out house;
and carry them home. We work
the wedge down, wondering
how deep this one,
and what shape,
turning up whatever
may be alive underneath, dark
moisture-loving bugs, worms. Cicada
husks hold tight to every upright,
and all around us the red-eyed wings
of noise sing the underworld, years
and years sucked from roots and spent
in a few days.
The stray cat, a snake
limp in its mouth, watches
from a safe distance,
so it believes.

We work
our way down the path,
one step at a time,
a plot of ashes at the end.

The hewn foundation disintegrates,
but the pathstones hold.
We raise the heavy ones
as best we can
and carry them,
singing,
down the ridge,
between us.

The Ceremony

During the night, when I hear the animals
walking along the stone walls under a full moon,
an irregular clicking, heavy, dark,
defining two sides of the house,

and in the morning, when the sun comes up
behind the blighted elms—then

oh well then the new floors arise, rippling
these bodies with light and shadow,
these walls, inside

the piesafe, frolicking
with white china.
On the new floors
window shapes

frame shadows: chokeberry
in the wind, delphinium
in the wind, dogs, cats,
friends, vases, stones—

a scroll
of creatures wrapping itself
around this house, gathering

at the glass to witness:
the woman in a grey sweat shirt, sneakers,
her skin clicking back and forth
through their reflections—
She is painting—

And the man, likewise, kneeling
on the new floor, his shirttail out—

Tomorrow

We stomp back and forth
over his head pleading.
That night

lightning cores the house.
Out of a deep sleep suddenly
we sit up, what is it—

a cat stealing breath, two dogs
seeding the house with their nails—

And then thunder, on all sides,

our white skins glowing like fruit,
our dark eyes,

and the bird, still alive,
under the house.

This Moment

The sun recedes one step at a time into itself until
the whole contour sits, this moment, on the horizon;
the reds collapse likewise,
overcome, it would appear,
by their own intensity.

Even though this or any part of it
is all there is

it isn't really. There's the whole realm of the other
in my thighs, in yours;
in the way they talk

about something else
always, erotic;

this is their love poem.
This is your shoulder
on which the red sun

steps down, your blousy sleeve
outlined, the full contour;
the one-button cuff

on the left
fastened;

the right, turned back; one hip higher
than the other. Your blue denim skirt
center front slit;
a watch pocket,
empty;

out of which you slip,
with crooked left forefinger,
the one thing
at sunset

excites me most.

In the Middle

The wind comes back. She sits
at the table, all the doors open.

Through the back screen she sees the flat stones step
across the yard, the four bales of straw
at the garden wall, the striped canvas lawn chair
blown on its side under the five elms—the woods
on the hillside beyond, glimpses
of the next ridge over, hazy.
The wind is in the heavy foliage, a flock

of shadows: it scares up: it settles back: the bells
catch it on the other side of the house.
Even in the middle

of the summer she can hear the cold.
The wind rises to a slow whistle
in the kettle as though it were coming
through the walls. At dusk
it's the house sitting there
in the middle with a cup
in its hands, not her.
She can see it

as from the garden: the house cups
its windows in the corner
as though the light within
were always on, signifying
most clearly at dusk,
palm to palm. She
approaches,
up the slope, drawn
always by the way the windows seem to rise,

out of the ground, to eye level, the house
kneeling down so that one can look in.
The light gathers

its colors from its source,
from the rough wood of the walls
and ceiling, from the way she sits there
at the table in the middle of it

as though it were hers, warm,
low to the ground, bells
in the wind. Fireflies appear
under the trees and on the slopes. Cassiopeia
rises over the lip
of her cup, low
in its sky.

Stars and Their Legends

Following the break of each wave and the surf
a thin surge of pink water
up the beach face at dusk,
the upwash, or swash
as some call it—

Legend says that we have
knowingly or not
left a footprint there

over which, this moment,
a sea gull hovers, taking bread
from a lifted hand.

The bird's ribs, caged
in light, our fingers,
inside each limb
a bone splinters

into light.
                    The sun, the moon,
the marsh grass in its full dimension—

The dunes, the darker foreslope
rolling over, the plunge—

The down tide terrace
in purple, deep purple,
and the sandbar, a thin
skim of light, mauve,
all the way out
to the shoaling waves,

no other person in sight.
What would we call ourselves?

The heavens say we perish
like a bird
into the air,
                                        a turbulence
where once we fed. And so

it happens, each hungry face
passes over the rolling surface
of the water at dusk, sliding

out of sight, stars
taking the place.

The Window

Imagine the phases of the moon, new to full
  only speeded up,
one second nothing there in the window,
just the snow storm, the next
a whole ball

flattening on impact with a deep thud. You leap
from your chair to the window and look out—

Given the drift the stunned body
is too close

at first for your startled eyes to take in;
globes of light go back the other way, full
to nothing, and out of that
the first clear impression

of the bird: lying wings outstretched in the snow.
You wonder whether or not it is still alive—
the window that clear now between you.
You have time only for its dark eyes,

still open, the yellow crest,
the particular grey breast and wings;
and then for the impression

disappearing quickly
as the snow falls
after it has flown, a hush

of other things flying in the dark.

Local Weight

Five days a week the school bus tops the hill
at 7:30 rattling
the dishes,
the windows

as it slams past; and every night, after dark, the cat hangs
on the window screen, featuring its claws, yellow eyes
off to the side, always
the same side. Other influences
on my posture come

from single instances, often
at dusk, a dangerous time—

the groundhog composed,
one foot up—

                                        Rain on the skylight
fits the moment like a helmet, my ears
are inside the sounds of grazing cows,
poised among the unseen.
The darkness yields only

the nearest tree, which continues
to grow at all angles,
to the sounds of grass tearing;

and a groundhog,
right front foot raised,

its weight the only body I have.

Pulse

A pond, fringed around by bullrushes, and swimming in it,
in yet another circle, a black dog, snapping every third
  breath
at insects. The inner ring of algae parts, swirls, re-forms,
even the wind seems green. The bullrushes sway.

The arrow-shaped cedar isolated on the hillside above
  the pond,
reflected in the clear middle, upside down, rippling—
it's as though the Indians are still here, at the moment
watching, black rocking with blue green.
It is pointing to the spot

where I enter the water, hot, sweaty,
the cold mud suddenly

frightening underfoot.
At eye level the tall flies land on the surface,
blue tails up, drifting with algae.
There's another level beneath that,

where the water is cold in pockets,
going out in short bursts
and then re-forming. Sky,

water, skin, each shifting through the day like a shadow,
layered, changing, the colors lengthening.
At some point my own blood enters in,
a leech on the top of my ankle,
I watch that too.
Under the surface

the sunset grows in tall stalks
of watery light, as though my legs
had come up suddenly under me,

I'm floating;
can see

in the way the shadows move, from the within,
deepening, each insect

is waving to me,
I am waving back.

DIVIDING RIDGE

It takes all day but finally the last two things
strike together, if not for the last time.
A clear silence appears

and deepens. In an intimate downhill fold of the land
a small windless pond backs light
at sunset, absolutely,
a glacial plain;

the proportions among the surrounding hills, trees,
   pastures
adjust accordingly. And then, again, nothing

moves. The sycamores in particular
seem reluctant to appear
in this diminished form;

not one thing will risk being mistaken.
It seems that only then can the last light slide off

leaving your hand to itself,
one finger earth, the others
water, air, fire,

and the thumb,
oh there's no word for what the thumb now
signifies. Not silence, not darkness,
not even the absences;
none of that, or any other.

Welcoming the Season's First Insects

Each with its own language, contingencies,
catalogues, instructions. When I imagine
all the creatures living within me,
within one cell of me,

I become a sun. All the midges
hanging over all the meadows

swarm within me, becoming one sound.
I sit here like a wishbone
in the garden's late light,

early spring, the sun's
tuning fork. The ants

ornament my skin in a line. Small
by reason of the great distance
between them and my eye

they carry me off. The weight
of their feet

sings, bless us,
we've made it
this far.

Kneeling at Easter to the Season's First Bloodroot

for Cia White

Eventually one spring enough ground was turned,
a windstorm occurred at the right moment,

the rest we piece together. Even if a human
had been here he could not have seen
what was rising
from the earth

and traveling by cloud east southeast over two ridges,
to a large stagnant pond—
owned by a man named Connors—

nor could anyone have seen it reappear,
out of the rain, as algae.
No one was here

when the grasses first appeared, or the whales.
No one was here long before that, the sun
circled and drilled, sparks leaped,
a bolt of lightning forked,
the earth was cooling,
one cell became two.

On the Day of Balanchine's Death

The light lifts one ridge after another, rowing the sun
out to sea. In the high pastures, on the near hillside,
the dark cedars perform, pulsing

a few last times at the edges,
in their tall shadows.
On the horizon, one ridge up
another down, the red sea
of light parts, color jumps
the world fast—

leaving ponds
in its footprints,

tribes of cedars standing by like spears.
Once they were dancers, loved
by those they astonished.
Now it is their turn.
They gather at dusk each to a cold station
under the stars, dark shapes without wind.
As the last light unravels into the distance
several final colors come loose
and wait on point

to follow. At the edge of town
early the next morning
the light is flat

all the way to the horizon.

Modigliani's Last Portrait of Jeanne Hébuterne

At the appropriate place in her face
the wild forlorn Jew has planted

her eyes, without pupils, blue seeds,
the roots pointed in, as though he knew only
one color, a whole picture tinged

with the blue growing from within her—
she's talking, one can believe, with the fetus.
It's fair to say that at this point a ghost
has entered the picture, stepping

from one color to the next, bending
her body as though space occupied
his fingers, time
was a color he could see—
a purple

taking the blue of her eyes yet deeper. Finally
they are all pupil, that opaque; every shadow
is derived, beautifully, of them.
They seem to know

that he is dead soon,
before the child,
and upon that, she too,
by her own will.
Everywhere

they turn takes root.

Monet

Open Window

Its first responsibility, deliverance,
is assumed in the second, framing;
it takes the wayward inexplicit world
and makes it suddenly mischievous,

snow kicked down
by a slight breeze

or a squirrel. Light is the special grace
to be sure, but the effects are our own:

a solemn drop out of nowhere
spreading across the surface,
the buried creatures rising,

often grandly. He watched the light work
from the top of the trees each morning down,
and felt it roll over in his shoulder each night,
leaving from the ground up; he watched it

in the hills, the waves, the stacks,
that same movement,
rolling over,

of release; the world full
of its tall servants
to the acts of light.
In his old age, enfeebled,
he went deeper still into his shoulder
for a longer reach—loved ones gone,
eyes failing,
he answered war

by expanding the size of his lilies;
the buried shapes and colors rising;
and then after the war, in his eighties,
blind, in despair, by again expanding,
flowers, flowers.

Closing

More than two men were needed to porter the last
canvases.
He would hurry ahead, as his old body allowed,
or hang back:

Over the humpbacked bridge his favorite view of the
grand panels
being moved out through the gardens each day to the
pond.
Given his eyes and all they had seen
water alone made sense now—

no surface, the light sinking,
slowly. Fewer and fewer colors,

each lasting only a few seconds, a few minutes;
the beloved realm of our bondage; he fell down
the hole of each flower—

the one come he knew
to take the first impact
of light, to mediate
its withdrawal—
working furiously

for seven years; often up at night, pitched high,
in a rage, wanting to burn the monsters; haunted

by what he was trying to realize.
Each changing shape was the same, every knot
that appeared had to be untied, there was no water,
not even, finally, those waning effects of light;
the dissonances grew ever more beautifully faint,
disappearing. The secret

he once said in happier times
is in not using black—
his last months spent thus,
the great panels gathered
around him in the dark.

Ars Poetica

for Robert Hazel

Whatever Happens

I quit calling

when they start to move
and watch them gain the ridge—

they come from the meadow below,
one behind the other, in profile.

It's when the calves forget (oh
how the calves keep forgetting!)
that I call again and again.
Evenings I do it, and call again
in my sleep, I dream sounds
of grass tearing.

I love
to sit on a rock in the cedar meadow,
the black cows around me—each at her distance—
some grazing, others staring back at me.
It is here they fatten.
Whatever happens

there's one who comes closest,
and even closer still:
the large black skull,
the jaws moving sideways,

a small bent version of me
in her eyes.

The proposition
is whatever I make of it.
I could even say, and make the case:
she's ready in her innocence for me

to kill her now
if I am.
The cedars will agree
whatever happens.

On the way home, making my neck as long as hers,
I imitate her shoulders, her heaviness
in the way I walk, arriving
slowly—

Moonlight

The great clapper of the sun disappears,
the bell swings up, red
ringing out to purple,
soon it's dark enough.

Black cows move slowly
on white legs, heads down,
a big moon rises.
From the far end

of the meadow a wind brings its light
by way of tall grass
into the oak wood

here—it rises up their trunks, out along
branchlets, dripping from new leaves.
Wet from a recent rain the moonlight
slides and bounds—
what is it

travels in the sound of earthgrass tearing?
In the bell, stars loosen,
a tinkling,

how many years ago
now?

The Eye

The weather turns on the creature, inside,
before her time. There is nothing either of us can do
but follow—north, then northeast at the line fence
and out along the far ridge. I find the fetus,
hoofprint in the creek bank, eye open
in the moonlight, steaming.
Whole days pass

in the shape of cows, the light grazing
back and forth, black and white
in the pasture here

and the fetus, having slipped, keeps falling,
slowly now, into every part of the field.
Whole days pass, white faces circling
the eye, closer,
so that each night

the moon is brighter, drawing me back—
the fetus calling to its twin. The mark
of the long head and the curve
of the body form a question

dotted by the eye, open, and that
by the moon, always full

in the bull's eye.
The cows,

heads lowered, chew
in the dark and stare,
and again,

something like them, pulsing
in the next circle out—

The Ear

In the late light of winter trees
the space between things expands and
overtakes them, shadow

movements the most conspicuous
(but hardly the only) agent.
In the ensuing darkness a grid

is implied, the work of the world continues;
though only a tiny portion is within human range,
and all of that a mystery,

a neighbor does call his cows;
you do listen—
                                        One of you
remembers certain things and forgets
others with such instinct they seem

no longer interchangeable, the moment
given form—

Is it you or he?

He calls again.
This time the cows come.
You write all this down.

Now comes the hard part.

Again he calls, again you listen, again
the space expands

including each cow in line, the spaces
between each sound, your feet, thus included,
then the glowing last light of a whole body,
in whatever posture, finally

the ear, the ear, waiting
for the last sound
among animals at feed.

First Snow

Before dawn the barred owl spun
in its shape like a leaf, flew straight
from the ridge woods behind the house
at the dark window

and kept flying. The storm
fit inside the two eyes
perfectly, lighted

as they swirled toward me,
wings everywhere. There

at a kitchen window in Kentucky,
a cold goblet of water in my hand.
I saw winged eyes in the moonlight.
It was snowing.

Our Fall Was into Forgetfulness

We see them only
when they surface
but what we see takes us
down: the great grey whales
in their instinct, the long
undulating dream of nature
from the Bering Sea south:
they rise up heavy for air:
their knuckled backs turning up
out of the brine like water wheels
three slow times before they dive:
the sun-etched arrows of their tails
unfolding momentarily against the sky,
slapping water into light: then gone,
down again into the sea deep
within us.

Old Places

for Wendell Berry

When the sun reaches the flat rock
on which the cat sleeps
the heat dreams her.
It's as though she is
remembering something.
She stands up
and changes

shape. On the margins
of the yard gnats fly out
of the tall brown grass

brushing the light. The cat stretches as she
enters the shadow of a tree, pulling her last leg in
slowly. She crosses the yard as though it were her
condition

to change shape with every move. She moves through
the shadow
of a tree as though it were within her, slowly.

She is the only thing
This is the only world
Each time she moves

it's as though something further is remembered
and brushed away. I'm in Kentucky, early August,
Harrison County. A mile and a half down the road,

in an old place between two ridges, there's a pond.
The slopes around it are dry, pocked
with the hoofprints of cows. The light
is flat, unrelenting, threatening

to slap, again, anything that moves.
The older a place is
the more ways it has

not to move.
The cows are there, some
in the water, dreaming themselves.
They are black. Already their legs are gone. Even
their tails have stopped moving. The longer they
  stand there
the blacker they become. This is only the world.
Sometimes they are not there at all.

It's as though they open all the way
to the end of something and I follow them

until I cannot move

Sleeping on the Bank of a River

Something is come up deep inside him, nibbling
at his lids, drawing the blood
back. From flesh

it takes his color
elsewhere. He has his hands

behind his head, his eyes
are open, he is staring
at the ceiling. His eyes

are blue canals, the lids
are the only thing about him
that moves. They shift,

a lock at a time, passing him through.
His whole body opens
back and away. It's as though something is

bleeding him. The longer I look at him
the less I would call it, white
is not so close to absence

as he is when he sleeps.
It is his sleep

staring at the ceiling now,
in the form of his body.
I am trying

to say exactly where we were when his eyes closed,
opening
on the inside and we are there, in the bend

of a river. He is dreaming
the eyes that dream him. Everything
is clear

again. He has left his flesh
sleeping, to be watched.
Around the bend boats come.
The river is old
and full of blood

He forgets even that
and the sleep deepens

A Stillness

From here you can see the herds
come down from the mountain.
Like loose rock they pile up
at the river.

Then break loose. The first one.
Then the others. Whole herds plunge
through the water. You can see the men
gathered in the pass with their spears
to watch. Already they are waiting
thousands of years.

And then the trees come. Birch and spruce
to the river bank. At some point
the men enter boats.
You see them

with their spears raised.
You see whole herds churning
blood, until there is none.
The water is water

again. A stillness.
You can see it rise to the surface
again. Like the moon.
As though no one
were watching.
All this time

the trees hardly move.

The Rider

Even in the middle of the fall I knew that someday
(if I survived) there would be a moral
to the story—not that the beast
survived too (it did,
though damaged),
not that I suffered
as much as it did
(I suffered more,
that doesn't matter)

but a full account
of how it all happened—

For generations we slept on warm stones, venturing
no farther than we could walk, carrying no more
than we could run with, gathering at dawn
along the ridges, in the passes,

to watch them graze—
each father whispering to his son

closer, closer. When the first man
took the first horse, he seized
the whole horizon by the mane.
The tall trees began to fall, the herds.

And then there were small houses
all along the way
to the big one

here on the top of the hill.

Traveling by Moonlight

When the mountain exists only as bells,
cattle grazing in the fog,
or higher up, on the tropical side,
as the sound of water falling,

the crater paths leave the rim
from either side and descend

like the hopes of those who follow
them, appearing and disappearing
in the roiling fog.
One flower survives.
The birds stand, one leg
banded, facing the weather.
Everything we understand about them
is written down, dated, mapped,
but who knows where they came from,
who knows where they are going. Sometimes
the fog takes them and keeps them,
even after it has gone.
                                        Then

the sky clears, then the wind follows,
then the whole island emerges, even the part
beneath the surface, and stands

on one leg, motionless, cone-shaped
light flowing out of the crater
and down the sides, green to blue
as it goes to sea.
                              The moon
comes here, or so it seems,
to sleep. At night, when the crater is full
of shadows, it's as though the moon

awakes again, overhead,
to watch. I find myself listening
to my footsteps in the red ash
as though someone else makes them,
a long time ago.

Adam's Love Song

Out of nowhere a great loneliness settles
into his chest. All he can hear
is his own heartbeat. Day after day
the pastures go off into darkness
and return without her,

nothing for him
to do but sit there

until he has forgotten even why.
Finally he is lonely enough,
his silence echoes.

I am here

he is saying
to some other
he can't yet see

Where are you?

Tall grasses quicken toward him
in reply, and then again,
something else—

He jumps to his feet and looks around,
the first inkling

of his features
becoming distinct—
two eyes, a nose,
a mouth

in which time
is about to sing.

The Relinquishments

After quarreling with everything in sight the heat hovers
around the edge of the pond and then subsides,
an audible vapor over the surface.
We enter a change of light, or is it

wind—a buzzard, overhead, storm clouds behind him,
   tightens
his circle on the subdued sun. For several minutes

rain pocks the steaming surface of the water,
anticipation builds. The sun, when it breaks, shatters

and roils—
                    What is explained by all the theories
put forward to date? I see the light
in its great waves
of relinquishment,

the transparent concentric spheres it passes through,
the vapors, the planets, the drops of water;
the light riding its circles within each current,
inside each bubble; I see it

break apart, the fingers elongating, flashing
loose.

Traveling

You need something you love that you can strap
over your shoulder; and a feel for what goes.

A father might carry in it a black stone
he and his son held in their clasped hands
walking back from the beach. Whatever

he would need were he to find himself
perched all night in an old tree,
or asleep on his mother's grave,
listening

to her heart beat through the hole
he saw her make there
when he was a child.
Certain stars

can help you know where you are:
they collapse in on themselves:
the mother's eyes

are still open, she is still motioning
for me to leave the room.

The Child

A few white birch
on the hill slope

step forth in the twilight, the grey woods
fall in line behind them. They take what is left
of the light and walk it a white trunk at a time
toward me—the darkness comes like parents

appearing behind them. It takes
the thin white trees from behind
one at a time

and comes on.
When it gets to me
the heavens are out, falling,
and the child is gone.

Fireflies cluster like stars
on the dark wet road
where I run.

Stopping on the Edge to Wave

> . . . light is on the edge—the last thing we know
> before things become too swift for us.
>
> —C. S. Lewis

The scene always takes place
at the gate, outside the wall,
and the assumption always is—

I can no longer even remember.
It's more a condition, like light—
Our condition always is

That I have the key
That you have the key
That we know what we are doing there

or here or anywhere. There is no key.
We stand atop whatever we can find
to climb up on, arm in arm,
peering over the wall.
There is no wall.

What is it then?
What is it we hope

to see on the other side? The vacant
streets lined with buildings. Nothing
moves, there is no color. Over the cobblestones nothing
moves, there is no sound. Behind the brick walls nothing
moves, as if we'd stopped off
in a photograph
on our way—

Where?

There is no where
and no when. As in a picture
of such emptiness, as if to speak
of such emptiness—nothing moves

at the center.
It is the light.
There are no sides.
The light falls

from the buildings into the streets
and keeps falling.
What more could we have
come all this way to know, hoping
to find our way

back to the room
of flowers, the bed,
the familiar stories? Everything

on the edge is familiar
where nothing is

the last thing we see,
like this light,
before things get too swift
for us. We thought we were

alone and indeed there is no other.
It is the light waving back.
We thought all things
change and indeed

there are no streets, no buildings.
The light falls
on white egrets
next to black
cattle grazing. The pasture falls

down to the sea. The light
has come all this way
bearing us with it. Each morning
at our backs the crater, each night
the sea. We are farther back
than we know. Nothing

does move—
in the form
of a white bird
it lifts off
and flies away
into itself

taking us with it, light
and then dark and then light
again, farther than we can see—
The sky
empty—

from

The Mother on the Other Side of the World (1999)

The Buffalo

crossing the yard to the old wall
I'm drawn along a circle
through each thing a full moon
seen over a considerable area of the earth
including the vast oceans rises
and walks down the wall
and through me
in the evolving white shape of a cat
for years these stones lay afield
gathering his footsteps even the clicks
sound old and have come a long way
his fur slipping through my hands
what did my ancestor hear
upon seeing the Shawnee step into
this moonlight with a small stone taken up
and shaped to his use what did the Shawnee hear
when the gun was cocked where did the sounds go
when the buffalo were slaughtered
were they fixed in time
or were they freed
into the real world mistaken
for snapping twigs or distant
thunder or history at night
when the small creatures walk this wall
isn't it the same gravity audible
the weight of each thing settling
defining the size of its earth the dead
clicking along in the moonlight with us
great silences in between
and within each of them
the dwindling herds

thundering back and forth
far and then farther away
the dwindling gunshots and screams
we shot them from trains for sport
we ate their tongues

Moonlight

on the railing of the circular stair
it climbs the first two flights
and finds its occasion pausing
at the silver pitcher
on a windowsill the moonlight
parts its lips in the wind
organdy curtains kiss back
its face now a pasture shaped
by old oaks and maples and
their elongated shadows
as it ascends the final flight
the moonlight hides here
and there behind bars
awaiting I come to see
the top of a blond head
visible just above the rail
and its elbow a figure
emerging the moonlight becomes
a crooked arm cocked up thin bare
hand to forehead in astonishment
a glimpse of white T-shirt
and then the whole a bed a rug
a table an unlit lamp chairs
two windows billowing white
shadows moving the moonlight now
is in the dark trees outside inside
in attic shadows not moving moonlight
awakens upside down with sleeping bats
whatever it touches
has its hand to its stunned head
it has come too far
seen too much

it's his mother
with her great womb
of otherness turning his
hand over palm up then the back
with its hairs veins liver spots
flexing his fingers untying
his shoes everything
each does is to the other
neither of them can help it
she's in the breeze moving
the rocker all about
on the hardwood floor

With Deer

with horses you can move the beam of your flashlight
from one to the next you can draw their legs
with deer there's usually a mother
you hold the beam very still
and not for long
behind the two
down the slope at the far reach of the light
four others appeared at the edge of the woods
so as not to frighten them away
I turned off my flashlight and waited
for my eyes to adjust
so as not to be there any longer
they were gone
leaving behind the rope hammock
among the five elms the red roof of my studio
a garden hose one of the dogs coming
around the side of the house
the moon at that moment

Hawkbells

hawks valued more
for their hunting
than their flight
are called birds
of the fist they
work from trees
and fence posts
in swift dashes
and twists often
close to the ground
falcons valued more
for their flight
are called birds
of the lure they
work in open fields
from a high pitch
above the quarry
diving and swooping
when you tame a bird
of prey for sport you
are said to man it
from hawk houses
and mews you work
with gloves tethers
hoods and bribes
a bird of prey
on the wrist is
a watch her
talons time
she examines you
as closely as you
her with this difference

you belled her wanting
flight always to return
to you you turned
yourself into a what
would you call it
to hood a bird
on the wrist
you must pull
the knot tight
with your teeth
a smile maybe or
threat even a kiss
whatever the promise
the bird says bird

Washing My Cup in the Last Light

I bend forward already knee-deep
in the pond watching my hand change
underwater at eye level
the perfected work of the sun's moment is
crosshatched rippling tall blades
of marsh grass and their shadows
on the narrow instrument of any one blade
ten winds play the shadows like keys
nothing here inside its riff
is upside down or backward
from the hillside above
the last light watches
a dry flat rock sitting
on the dirt like a teacher
his thistles crossed
bugs flying up and down
his shins

Yet to Be Named

a dappled gray gelding at the edge of the woods moved
into the beam of my flashlight rocking his head back and forth
smearing his visage he knew a lot more than I did
that was as much sense as I could make
of the goings-on down there namesake
the strange word on my ear
from within the woods
came the sourceless whinny
that went with his looks
the farawayness of it began
and circled out and back to
its beginnings within me
too the blood rose
right out to the surface
as a loose horse evolved up the slope and into my light
and across the exhausted garden toward me strutting
throwing its red head rolling all kinds of eyes
my light
caught its eyes
its red eyes
doubled the bet
and threw it back
a large broad-breasted mare
I turned the light on myself
she came even closer
all the way now up
only the rock wall
stood now between us in the middle of her broad forehead
a white diamond marked the spot where if I dared I'd put
my small hand
dares had gotten me
there so up I stepped

and into the moonlight
lots of hips shoulders eyes
I sent them up and down
the full length of the stone wall
back and forth over the tricky places
this took a while
in the pads of my feet
and in the stride of my legs
I returned to life and played
the clicking stones whatever
it took to keep her
moving at my side every
now and then a snort
a whinny until
she was gone
replaced after the passage of time
by a sleek stray dark gray cat
yet to be named leaping up
as I leaped down hopscotching
through my echoes and my light
toward my hand

Kneeling

a young deer running up and down
a wire fence searching
for a way through a way under
a roadside fence only a few yards
of shoulder no one in sight
the road's emptiness expanding until everything
within hearing stops turns
toward the creature's fate
one meadow up the mother stops
alert to the distant rumble of a car crossing
the bridge to the distant screams
of children playing there
to her young
searching the near shoulder up and down
for a way through for a way under slipping
into the ditch bolting onto the road and then off
along the fence again frail legs
weakening
the approaching car stops
I switch off the motor
at the first station
of the ensuing silence the flat sun broadsides a barn
in the next meadow up turning its whiteness toward
me opening its black door suddenly the atmosphere
thickens rank rich the fences go on alert
each thing holds fire the encircling incense
of manure the spiraling chant of a silence
full of whirring crickets
its message fire itself
in the backlit fields
of ironweed each plant a purple torch burning
inward and all together falling the long shafts

of themselves each head bowing
in a crown of light kneeling
into the sounds of
insects swirling
and darting
in the low light
long after the young deer is gone

Ars Poetica

the way a fox slips into one side
of your headlights and carrying his tail
(like a pen running out of ink) slips
out the other—

This Kiss

for a good part of the school year the bus arches
over the rise in front of our house kissing the brakes
in the dark
when I'm not there to watch
I listen
each year the regular driver handles
the bus in the same way day after day
almost exactly and you can tell a lot
about the condition of the hilly curvy road
the bus-sound accelerating and braking
we hear it oh how long less than a minute
if I miss seeing the school bus
in front of the house whooshing past
in a long second I usually catch the taillights
topping the next hill up the road
in the past with running lights
but not this year
we live way back far out
the driver
this year kisses the brake
as she tops that hill
a secret among us
that only a poem could celebrate
well no you and I do independently
and when we compare notes together
the new driver turns off the inside lights too
in years past there was a one-trick carnival
at 7:06 yellow running lights Ferris-wheeling
the long yellow cab of mostly empty seats all lit up
a roller coaster midway on a three-rise roll
now with only headlights and taillights
there's something otherworldy at that moment
and much more urgent a little spectral at times
I hate that creeping in
without moonlight there's no yellow none
I've never understood how long those rides are

or how desolate those two kids
one way up here and the other way over there
in there in the dark now so dark that even in moonlight
you wouldn't know they were in there unless you knew
if I say one more thing I'll make myself sad
such are my thoughts outside your cracked door
you're in there clicking away I've just stopped by
to say whatever comes out of my mouth
this kiss blown through the opening

Names

the graying balding fellow tall a little
stooped a shy smile supporting-role mentality
after ten plus comfortable years
together at functions and on elevators
what possessed us to lean forward
that time and exchange names
to lean back embarrassed
then and thereafter
no excuse now for not knowing
who the other was
look out
the next time I saw the man
I avoided him
and the next or
was it he me now
soon I disliked the very sight
of him and wondered how long
before he retired or died
and he too
with me maybe
who knows
everything got that way
I had to change jobs
go friendless without being aware of it
I got a divorce
I'm not blaming that poor innocent man
I'm not blaming anyone
I'm telling how
I got here watching the obits
for our forgotten names

A Second Place over the Mountain

an early morning fog battery dead
her bumper kissing a stranger's
in the McDonald's lot
both hoods raised
here we go he says toasting
his large coffee one long levi leg out the door
the other booted foot on his pickup throttle
exactly
she hers high-idling
each windshield steaming
the charge building
he unhooks his cables and throws them
into the big homemade box in the back
when she kills the motor for the test
he checks her oil for good measure
wiping the dipstick on his pant leg
she has a second place over the mountain on the coast
he's acting as though he suspects something of that sort
as a three-person line forms at the newspaper stand
as other passengers from the Greyhound
hold the door for each other
as the fog lifts a little
doubling the size of a red sun
she lights a cigarette and rearranges things
on the front seat and rolls the window down an inch
to leave with him a chin-raised kiss
a shoulder-high screwing in of the old light bulb
as she goes that's her wave slipping
into a break in the traffic
bye-bye or follow me
appearing and disappearing
in her swinging blond hair

Getting Naked

I had grown tired of hanging around
on her string acting like a kite
I had fallen was under the table
naked acting like a bird
she crawled in with me
took off her sweatshirt her boots her levis
smiling and flapping our wings at each other
we negotiated for who was in charge
she sought to show me it was a disgrace
for birds
to wear clothes
she was cute and wise
like the wind taking shape
in our skins

Love

what are your standards for conferring trust
would it help you to know them have you been
too quick to trust or too slow if you must err
which error is preferable
do you seem protective of this subject
or otherwise protective protective
of what pretending sleep pretending
whatever bonded to what's beyond control
especially to what's happening behind your back
you must have heard your love preparing
to slip out of bed or so you thought
you must have heard it actually happening
felt your side of the bed sink soundlessly
or as it happened to me I in my cot
on one side of the room felt
my side of the room sink
you must have lain there
for a period of time a roach
a wall for companionship deciding
which was worse waiting for her to return
or going to hunt for her and you must
have decided to hunt for her and you must
have found her wherever she was
whatever she was doing

Her Fingertips

all those years
she could have been any age
not born trying to die her
hands would rise up around my face
as though they were my own
and only she knew what they were doing
tracing my veins drawing my blood
to the surface I knew only
that they were hands
and we loved many
of the same things
one cup in particular
fingers laced
palmlessly
the light
dividing
over her
body her body
enlightened with this
the part I love best
and this if I said more
she would shush me

Desire

turn toward me as you close the door
with advice where for instance
should my hands be within
your fragrance doing what
since you're just back
from adventure
lean closer
as soon as the opportunity arrives
so that your hair rocks
around one ear releasing
its scent and tell me
about your exploits
if I don't understand
show me
in the way you move first your hair
then the hand to look after it
and then some other body part
of your choosing at times in
accordance with my desire
other times your own

The Fox

the blind side
of the hill came through
an opening in the trees it opened
out into the pasture like light poured
from a pitcher we were waiting
to see what forms would evolve
thus the fox appeared gathering
its eyes in to drink
over both shoulders and
straight ahead everything was
gathered in it stopped in front of us
as though it saw
we were not there
not even a body
moved where would it go
for years we've watched this pasture
coming through that opening
in the guise of different seasons each
with its name it takes our eyes away and brings
them back blue and blue and again
blue these bodies mouths and thoughts
these conditions around them
when I am restless
I think it must be the fox
trying to come back
but it's a breath
on my face my neck
of old my heart
beating has come for each thing

Absence

by the end of the second day a toad
will have become cocooned in your hair
and the dogs will have banged in and out
their door many times following it
from room to room and across
the orange carpet into closets
the backs of closets
each empty night now
they will pass from room to room mere echoes
of their nails on the hard floors even the walls
seem to have forgotten us and each morning
after smelling the pellets of food scattered
around their dishes and turning away
in sadness they will come back
to lie down head to paw and to grieve
our absence gathered around
them in shrouds
only in their dreams
do they find themselves dogs again
the missing truck known
by its sound tops
the hill and they
are in the drive
barking at each other
as they always did

Home from the Hospital

the downhill winter trees stand sunset up
out of the ground strict bold salutes
claws of reddish light rake each
truck all the way down scoring
the bark one thing
after another arrives
behind her in welcome
she's back among them
her arms wrapped around her knees
first a phone pole
followed by a barn a pickup
a sauntering dog nose down
dark shapes lengthening
as they mount the trees
in front of her
slowly steeply
gray to blue
the woods grow more still
even the slightest breeze
reveals unnoticed leaves
unappreciated conjunctions
she feels her own shadow coming
before she sees it split
between two trees
half close half far away
both rising
unevenly peering into the shape-shifters
she sees the dog's yellow wagging tail
a squirrel or is it the field cat
moves come spring crystal insects
will whirl around in the last rays
everything seems to be watching
three slender blond stalks
catch fire especially the broken one
flat-lit seeds hanging down from pods
in a touch of breeze

Prayer for the New Year

here the acts of your hands this
winding and rewinding of a red thread around
one finger at the middle knuckle slowly figure-
eighting it to the next finger here
the acts of my blue eyes watching
and the dog twitch-running in sleep

Brother Prayer

with all the help
I've been able to muster
I can see three bodies drop
any minute now from one of those darkening trees
on the vast lawn the man first
he takes the fall with his knees is running
when he hits the ground
for the big house
next the two children as the twilight fireflies appear
the older girl followed by the faster boy
both reach the stone steps
at the same moment and stop
under the awning one step up
you'd think they'd close ranks
you yearn for them to hold hands
as they peer through the screen door
into the shadows sounds
come back dishes
being washed and put away
someone walks across the big hall upstairs
fireflies take up the evening under the trees
cricket-lace surrounds these events
and the blond children
opening the door

The Owl

how long was he there in the dark his ear pressed
to the next room and the next above and below
echoes echoing one sir
leading to the next
he was the namesake
however it came down
I see the child I was
with all his skin
clothed his back turned always
the same ear at the same spot on the wall
that was my place in the pecking order
obedience leading to eavesdropping
I listened for women there was this one
place I'll swear I could have heard a knife being drawn
across a piece of bread I was on the verge
of knowing whether it was butter
or jam there was another place
with more than one sound
an owl his forward eyes radiating
spinning a full dark circle
was it my mother who told me
the one who died
mournful sounds
from far off but not far enough
liquid at the bottom of the well
that was my way of climbing up
on the edge and circling
each of the owl notes
before being called down
mother what mother moonlight
lay on the hardwood a membrane
thin naked hovering

just above the surface
all of the owl notes
quivering on it
I'd leave the wall
I'd descend the stairs
in search of her
along the moonlit banister
I ran my surface hand
along her surface

Little Man

for a while I thought I still had a chance
to come out ahead wait
until he found me still there
the perfect soldier true
to the perfect salute wait
until he realized
what he had done
going off and leaving me there like that
and after a while I cried
well actually I didn't cry
I only wanted to
I was his little man
here's the dirty part
later when I tried to tell him
what had happened
when all I wanted
was very little nothing
I didn't dare let him see
what it was doing to me
don't don't don't
I told myself
don't hurt his feelings

Young Man Comes of Age in America

you would have thought it impossible to take a splinter
three-quarters of an inch long in the crease
of your thumb pad
and not know it
except for days afterward
there was a dull ache
in another part of his hand
and then for weeks an itch
he was afraid to look at it afraid not to
he pulled off the road
in the middle of the night
between Columbus and Cincinnati
hundreds of miles away the maps
slid from their shelf to the floor
and under the dash light he examined it
first one hand and then the other
he picked at it constantly
it began to fester
then backed off this went on and on
one day he was stacking firewood
with his father screaming
at him or vice versa
they were big holes now
in each other's gloves
or maybe they were both okay for once
when suddenly the splinter broke the surface of his skin
for the first time his fingertips felt something
to get ahold of his whole body shuddered
as he drew it out he was sobbing
his father's arms around him
maybe that once

Our Mother's Hand

was it raining
were we on the sleeping porch
under the tin roof
rain on a tin roof
I'm always reminded
never quite sure of what
am I right to see it as happening in a big house
who was it with my ear pressed
to the wall what was he listening to
his ear such a funnel
he was listening to the next room
and the next above
and below
to chambers
echoing within chambers
children were loose in the house
it was his job to hear them
whose room was it the one
he was in did he hear
bodies
rushing through the house
rain on the tin roof
how long was he there
was he ever elsewhere
and where is that

It Felt So Good but Many Times I Cried

depending on how brave I was
I would leave the cedar closet door open
sometimes only a crack
as little as possible
I would have to stop halfway in
waiting for my eyes to adjust
once I took off my pajamas
at that juncture usually I waited
in order to touch the fox
first you had to go into its face and ask permission
then you had to take its yellow eyes to the door
to the crack only when it knew where it was
were you free to run your hands up and down
the whole length of its fur your fingers spread
and to turn your hand over letting the wrist drag
to take the whole piece up to your face to smell it
or more exactly smell mother
I took that piece
into the darkest corner
her piece we called it
we got down into our own little place
just the two of us between coats sometimes
my blue eyes its yellow
among the dresses
I took off my clothes
I rubbed the red fox
and its missing body
into mine this limb then that
it felt so good but often I cried
I kissed its nose its eyes
I may even have stuck my tongue inside its mouth
rubbing fur back and forth across my face

over my eyelids many times over my eyelids
it felt so good but often I cried
and when I was ready I mounted it rode it
mother's fur was there right there
its missing body was there
entering mine and many other things
as well entering me it felt so good
but many times I cried

Final

the question concerns all the creatures living within you
you write your name in the appropriate place the date
already you're taking too long
already you're late and getting later
already your loved ones are leaving
already you've started over
already to no avail
if you knew how this subject of all subjects eluded you
would you know where to look for it
whether your name is written backward or forward
and those numbers what they mean
your hand the one holding the pen your mind
already your mind

Emerging Shadows at Sunset

a white egret on the shoulder of a grazing steer sits
in a slow pivot a compass facing the sun
the dogs come up short ears grow
tall in the grass
the mountains climb out
of the water again
the day leaving
its colors in the clouds
and then retrieving them waving
one last time in the near pass
then the far this light
and I exchange skins
in the rising darkness
as I enter the water all
color quits my body my
flesh is cold and white
my legs are going
without a sound
wherever I turn buoyancy
has a center gravity
floats much that I see
is out of sight shilly-
shally feet floor
the ocean imprint
I hear the moonlight
pivot hardly audible
through the dark

For My Mother on My Birthday Many Years after Her Death

they arrived in you that day like guests
to a party your tired arms and legs
your skin your senses even
your tongue simple now especially
the one finger and you
there to welcome
accepted their gifts
the sheets on your bruised stomach
and thighs the sounds
of cars on the wet street
the shapes of windows folding
and unfolding around the walls and across
the mirror across the ceiling
like scarves discovering repeatedly
your finger huge of a sudden
in the newborn's palm
folding and unfolding
the ties loosening
and so finally
your breath pulling
its waves throughout your body
who was this you thought you would know
this self this other stranger than
a night's dream
passing another
you'd never seen
on a street you'd never been on
and that portent of having known him
by his hand his closed eyes since before
your own mother was born

Requiem

two columns of survivors followed horses carrying
armed guards each wobbly line trailed by a nun
other nuns accompanied those needing help
one especially invoking the tableau
the woman her head bowed in sorrow
the man coming up behind her
brandishing his power
in whose behalf is seldom clear
only the sorrow is clear
she held her own bandaged hand up
to keep it from throbbing
with the other she signed in the weakest
Ed-uar-do the nurse said aloud as she wrote
waving away flies between each syllable
too weak to exercise with the rest
he sat on the bank of a latrine
next to the barbed wire fence
thinking he'd been left behind
and that night dumped his still-muddy hand
onto the wood floor between his pallet and the next
palm up this was a hospital seventy some prisoners
in one room three nurses and every other week
an old doctor for half a day a bunion specialist
at times an accumulation of spirits lifted off bodies
and hovered there too weak to escape
and Eduardo charted the drift the bank
the stagnant places
his whole family could be dead
he knew his sister was
when he called for water
his fever voice was an echo
an empty vessel bobbing
on the swell of protest
when he recited family names
flies buzzed in and out of his voice
and around in the dark the sleepless

others railed threatened threw shoes
and clothing
a white horse
glimpsed through a swinging door
signaled an official
coming in to see what all
the fuss was about

God's Overture

first it will increase in size
and intensity consuming Mercury
and Venus bringing the waters
on earth to boil then
it will collapse glow
dimly the moon will disappear
finally our sun will burn out hurling
through darkness as far as we
could have imagined forever
a whistling cinder
I forget how small
all of this set about with explosions
the real music of the spheres God's overture
my science teacher called it
and then things begin all over again
under pressure of starlight
and of its own gravity heaving
clouds of gas and dust slowly condense
cloud clusters thicken prefiguring planets
in the atmosphere lightning goes to work
and heat from a sun millions of years
it takes and millions more the smallest change
takes centuries
with the first boil steam
blankets the planet further warming
the waters in that wet heat
things acquire new
complexity along
the protracted shores
and inland seas
in the brackish marshes
a cooling off finally
comes and further
contractions the same
old same old foreshadowing
the cell where before had been only

random process repetition
occurs self-feeding bubbles rise
to the surface a small crater lake
fed by hot springs minerals
of all colors on the shores
and underwater the water deep
and still brownish green
smelling of sulfur
bubbles rise to the surface
and pop give off audible vapors
no one's there to hear or smell
after many years something
appears that reproduces
wherever water collects even scummy water
eventually things gather other things hide
and watch the situation eventually
explodes helmet in hand his sweaty
blouse hanging from his waist
a soldier in midthought knelt to cup it
from his own image anointing
himself one last time history
finished the sentence a period
at the base of his spine followed
as he spun and tried to stand
by its dot-dot-dots across his flesh
I know that young man's kin these words
echo him on notification of his death
his wife stillbirthed the fetus
was given to science that's how
I came to know about all the bubbles
rising to the surface and popping
and the rest of the story
I was thirteen
finding my way in the world
by hanging around after school
making myself useful
lore had it the human fetus
on the top shelf in the storage area off
the science lab was a relative of the teacher

all I was sure of was she liked me and I liked her
that was a lot in those days I climbed the ladder
in there to see if it would open its pickled eyes
many times in my imagination only once in reality
X witnessed Y at the top of that ladder already I was
curling into its equation avoiding
the dirty-picture guys afraid
of girls refusing to notice
except when I had a boner
that's what my friend Bill called it
after fondling myself for weeks
with my sister's panties
I ejaculated for the first time
Fall 1948 Glendale California
no idea what was happening
I slid to the floor knees to chest
making noises promising God anything
for the chance to start over from scratch

The Mother on the Other Side of the World

a yellow cat from the next field over hungry finds
her way to the feed bowls inside our toolshed atop
the deepfreeze our striped gray lets this happen
then moves low to the ground
into position crouching outside
staring at the only escape
too frightened now
to eat the stray too stares at it
neither can see the other
for the longest time
something dark emerges
almost audibly circles
of their silence their
motionlessness pulse out
into the greater commotions the spins and counterspins
including the entire backyard the neighboring fields
many horses the adjoining areas
each of us moving in God knows
how many different directions at once
these two cats one almost wild
the other almost domesticated
get their version of it
lined up perfectly
great longing compacted
their own little seesaw
the whole backyard seesaws
that mother on the other side
of the world
many fears
but only this one silence
the stray's tail was all I saw
of her when she got out of there
that night beginning the plot of this story
I was to see about that much of her
again the next night in my headlights
at the side of a narrow road

a half mile away
yellow eyes
echoing outward the darkness it was
gonglike and out there in the expanding middle
I was to see more and more of her
in the days to follow
she hangs out in a culvert
I pull off the road and climb down
with a plastic cup of food
emptying it out on a scrap board I took down there
if I've got time to visit I usually do
she stays at the other end of the culvert
as though she'd never ever come closer
sweet talk doesn't run her off
but she prefers quiet it seems
occasionally she'll have a dead mouse
or chipmunk prominently displayed
a gift for me perhaps or maybe
a reminder of the role
she allows me to play
she never lets me see her
lick herself or sleep

from

Praeder's Letters (2002)

. . . .

Note: A little less than half of this book-length epistolary poem, which has four sections, is included here. Full lines of ellipses, similar to the one above this paragraph, indicate where passages and/or whole letters have been left out. Postscripts are common, often unidentified as such. Each new letter is headed by a date and place.

JBH

from

section ONE

of

Praeder's Letters

1.15.1956/sjpr

/ Dear Billy my lad

Through channels as intricate as life
itself I have to hand a copy of Stylus
Thank you thank you   Indeed

I am not dead though more
I cannot say

                    You are God
bless you one of the three
people in the world who
conceivably could care

I sound intolerably grim
about it after all
it is a witty poem worthy
of your fine mind
                              & I am honored
to find my name attached honored
is hardly the word

                              but frankly
excuse me I am moved by this
deeply &
as usual
unable to express
myself forgive
me

            Thank you thank you but Billy
it does take me back your poem
hurls me back

with such emptiness
to our cold days in Lex the Toddle House
the Green Dome & Fetterman with his stinking
dogs
        Tell me how I fell into the house
of a weightlifter will you
                                        & Winston
with his ascots & chemistry set
The man actually slept in my bed
his beard each morning stuck up
into the fetid air
                            & Grant C
keeping his profile among the press
of students   I miss
the man
             But I have forgotten
the name of the lady in your peom
poem excuse me
                            though I do recall
her suave tongue & vaginal intensity

& her squalid mind
which I now forgive

                                Poetry indeed
redeems you are far the better poet
Billy I could not have written
such incisive lines for that dark lady
I being the blackest spot in the pot
Thank you/

                If the day
were longer my memory
better I would try
to account for myself
since I left Lexington your town

of sweetness & light but
it is no story anyway
what the hell

                    I never
had business in a university
not for a minute as I am sure
you well know

                    I was
in NYC for a while worked
as a bellhop fill in
the blanks

                    Am now
in the Coast Guard
again & at my own request
in San Juan where
at the moment I sit
with newly bought pad & pen
in a cafe

                    They speak Spanish
here which is fine with me
shake hands over my head
which isn't

                    I am not Gauguin
nor as the saying goes
was meant to be

                    but it is true
Billy that I have bought this pad
& pen on the strength
of your peom

there I go again
poem Get a hold of yourself
Praeder

On *your*
strength it is These
are the first words
I have written in who knows
& who cares

SJ
is no Hawaii thank God
Latins seem to be in my fate
& there are certainly worse people
in the world

Dignity
is upheld here
by pissing in the streets
Their honor is agreeable
to me
even if they do
shake hands over my head

& what more can one ask
in this life

I quit
this else I begin to sound
like Ernest Hemingway
your affection for the man
notwithstanding How Ezra
tolerated such a child even
for the purpose of teaching him
is beyond me

but then Ezra
usually is

The truth is
& it always comes out always
I had in mind with the purchase
of this pad & pen not simply
to thank you for your elegant
& generous dedication but to make
of the same stroke an effort
of my own

A Dimensions #3
sort of thing
cafe hand wrestling
in the colors of Jacob with the angel
faint afterimage
if I do not enlarge
myself insufferably
of the spirit of the dead watching
no caps
you know the kind

and offer
it to your fine magazine
More of that later if more
indeed there is ///

I am a radio operator
I work 32 hours a week
I have enough money
I drink some
I fuck some
I read some
mostly history

I stalk barracuda
the only danger
I enjoy

Well
that is done with
& it didn't take long
What now

I am as shy
as a young thing my hands
go to pieces

Your poem
Praeder you even spelled it
right now
to it

Is this
any way to write
an old friend
Is this any way
to do anything

Imagine here three asterisks
& an ampersand signifying
a lifetime spent between
that last sentence
& this

In which of course
I completed a serious study
of Ezra
Have you read
Section: Rock Drill

It is no Pisan Cantos
but then what is

                                    & even wrote
my dissertation   The total light
process a single Chinese character
scratched with a hunting knife
on the side of my Zippo lighter

Tell them about me
at Harvard I'm sure
you will

It isn't Latins in my fate
it's the sea

                        I will probably end
up mesmerized by agony staring
into the eye of a flying fish
Then the long last header
into the brine

                              If I can ever
overcome my embarrassment //

* * *

Dear Billy   It is late
at night there are rats
under my bed within the hour
the whine of garbage trucks
in Calle Sol
                          & there is no
poem   There is no
poem

          Van Gogh wanted to kill
Gauguin with a razor but cut
himself instead

& sent
the issue to a whore
It loves to happen
Before sleep that night
swaddled in the bandages
of his next self-portrait
he placed a lighted candle
in the window in hope
that she would come

Can you believe it
I can

Enough
enough I send a verse
instead   Beware of men
who use meter & rhyme
& other men's matter

Dimensions #3
(for Odysseus Adams me not dead)

There was this woman
Who lived in an ether of sighs
The devil lived in her finger
And Kinsey looked out of her eyes

Enough indeed   Write me
if this does not depress
you beyond repair

Love & kisses Paul

* * *

& who pray is this Baxter Adams
Have you finally become

the Maxwell Street Presbyterian Church
Got vocabulary cards in pocket
Wm. Baxter Adams would be bad enough
You are as insufferable as I am
& who would have thought it
Face it Billy
you are just Billy
even to those who love you best
Tell your grandmother I said hi
& be sure to collect your paper route
before the 10th of the month

The only hope for a poet
is to learn first to pick
his nose you know that
if you don't just ask

Paul

1.30.56/SJPR

Dear Billy & Billirenes

Why of course I know Kathleen
& a pox on her for not remembering
I knew I was never in Lexington not
for a minute
                    Remind her Billy
Baxter Adams if you please of that grim
blackguard who came to see her
in the hospital with Bracket

Now do you remember
                                        I said
not a word hung at the door
one foot on top the other
like a minor Dickens come
upon a sweet shop window

& said not a word

Pray what could I say
in the presence of such
beauty such suffering
She had misused her arm
on a motorcyle if I am not
mistaken
              which impressed me
mightily
              though I would never
for one minute have admitted it
never

        Her brother was there
or if he wasn't I imagined him

& in addition to my general
embarrassment my silence
was due to no uncertain dislike
of the man

                              He was not only
better educated & better looking
than I
                    but more intimate
with the young lady

for which I will never
forgive him /

                                  All these warts
& elbows confuse & irritate you
I am sure as well they should
you forgetful hussy

But the awful truth is I am
at deep heart a rather simple
& sentimental fool
                                             & I
had rather confuse & irritate
than embarrass

                                        To embarrass
is the only unforgiveable sin

I am sure you have had your fill
of congratulations & felicitations
so congratulations & felicitations/
There is only one thing I have
ever

wanted in this miserable life
from time to time I see it clearly
& even though infrequently admit
it to myself & that
hold on to your seats
is a wife

sovegna vos

                    Poetry
is the sole tolerable occupation
only because love is so
difficult   I was going
to say impossible

but given the occasion
that would be
in bad taste

                    Please
pay no attention to me
life is difficult enough
as it is

               Not even a wife
I often suspect since I am
sure the dignities of marriage
are beyond me
                         leave love out
of it you will have to sooner
or later anyway

but a mother
for my children
That this will never
come to pass is one

of the few recommendations
left for the world

                                        Enough
of this I had in mind ceremony
as I always do & lest you think
I am a fraud here my children
of sweetness & light is what
I propose to wit

                                    // BUT FIRST
forgive me there are poems at hand
first things first my selfish
schemes can wait I would never
forgive myself
                              though I am afraid
hermano I have hard words for your
young ears

                          This business about
taking the summer off to write
a navel ooops
the truth again as always outs
novel
        there now
Well it is

what
        Pure Kentuckiana
you are the most careful bastard
I have ever encountered more careful

than Grant C you are all so careful
It is why I left   Get your finger
out of your ass

If you will excuse
me for saying so you will someday have
to choose between being a paperboy
& a writer
& FURTHERMORE as Ezra
would say if you want to be a poet
you will have to make harder choices
still

I saw a man this morning
in Calle Sol his eyes swollen shut
from a beating   His young son
was with him hand in hand
It was impossible to tell
who was leading whom
not even they knew
I am sure

Take off from what
pray   Is writing a part of your life
or not   And a summer good God
Adams if I did not know you
to be brilliant but young
I would think you a fool
You might as well take the summer
off to play with yourself or make
mobiles for the crippled children
If you have a novel to write
you will write it & it will cost

you your life if it is worth
writing   Don't talk to me
about taking the summer
off

Which brings me to your
poem de Soutine   Lucky you
did not try to write about Gauguin
I would come to Lexington & crack
your young head

But even Soutine
who incidentally you vastly overrate
deserves better at least half your
mind and let's face it
a little of your heart
just a little
Billy

Have you ever
looked at his work
I think not

You are writing
about a man's struggle
for his integrity
& you seem hardly
aware of the fact

skimming
surfaces you suppose compelling
like one of nature's insistent
waterbugs   Leave waterbugs

to nature   You're an artist
Do you remember

                        & never
use the word rainbow again
never   Maybe in French
I don't know but you prove
no more able to restore the word
to English than Mr. Lawrence
the less said about the innocent
the better

                I sorely mistrust
anyone who hangs carcasses
in his room to watch them rot
but I have an inkling of what
such fits are about having
specialized in them most
of my life
                But you seem
to have not the slightest
a careful Kentuckian
with his finger
missing

              If I sound intolerably
arrogant it is because I am
but this is not a matter
of taste yours mine
or anybody else's

                     I am
surely the oldest living
thirty-two-year-old

maybe the oldest
living period
Surely

        What do you think
of me now Kathleen

And because I know you to be
a poet in the making one
of the two or three I have ever
known & I include all the books
in the Library of Congress
& know that you have no need
or want of delicacies
which are always lies always
leave them to your Kentuckians
& academics

                    I have
a 12th-century mind
best to face it

                    & WHATSOMORE
your handwriting is worse than
mine worse than the blind JJ
in the last mix of the Wake
Desist
        What do you mean you
gave your typewriter to Ducksoo
I thought surely he would be
president of Korea by now
if not the world   What kind
of self-castration is that
                            You
did not want to type de Soutine
as well you shouldn't the man

sucking the artist again giving
away his typewriter indeed   Don't
tell Orphan Annie about hard times
do everything for him or nothing
rent him a typewriter & pay the rent
only don't give Mata Hari or even Ezra
your typewriter

                                        Maybe you should
take the summer off to write a novel
after all

                    I'll get off your back
if you will you didn't lose a leg
at Argonne that's the trouble//

There is a word in Hawaiian   hanamai
it means literally work-sick
It is used with regards to fucking
mostly
                  excuse me Kathleen
but equally applicable to poetry
there not being nearly as much
poetry in Hawaii as fucking
or anywhere else
                                        Work
until you are sick & then
work some more Billy
There is no other way
It isn't the hours
it's where the words are coming from
& that is not something
Grant C or this new man
Harris will tell you

                                          Trust old Stanislavski
I love you well hermano but you are

a clod sometimes even
on your wedding night

This brings me to The Rope Walker
a great poem   Here you have gone in
& done your work instructed me
which is the least I expect
of you
        & moved me
which is the most

That the man who wrote
The Rope Walker wrote
in the same lifetime this
de Soutine business
boggles the mind
It is a work of near genius
there are no rainbows in it
you are writing from where
you live I honor you
You can have my typewriter anytime//

I'm not done with you yet Billy
Please stop maligning your magazine
immediately I know only too well
what the Hudson Review & those hounds
have to offer that Stylus does not
& it is why I prefer you absolutely—

Which brings me back
to my beginning
as everything seems to

                                Listen
if this sounds utterly presumptuous
just tell me I'll understand

But I thought maybe the two of you
would like to come down here

this summer
                    A honeymoon
or a vacation or however
you choose to think of it

I don't have a great deal
to offer but this is a tolerable
place one of the very few
There is sun
& beach & water
SJ itself is beautiful
the old city

                  I will get you
a place you need not worry
about anything except getting here
There are two rooms vacant this moment
on the next roof top over   I can see
inside them almost as I write
Give me the word & I'll secure it

               During the day
you will be left alone
strictly
           & at night we
will eat & talk & drink wine
we will read poetry to each other

                  As the spirit
moves us we will take
long walks

                  Just tell me
if I am a fool I will
understand

There are even several other
people here whose company
is no more trying than my own

What do you say

You can write your novel
here Billy on my typewriter

l&k p

2.12.56/SJ

Dear Billy Baxter Axter
il milgor fabbro lest we forget
or remember

The garbage trucks
are whining in the streets below
the lizards hang on the window
screen in front of my face
they have followed me around
the world & found me
not wanting sly & cunning

Odysseus all sunburst & cloudfist
ruined western culture
& not even Ezra
understands it

Listen
you constipated bugeyed
cocksucker I feel this moment
like an old San Juan whore
sequaciously into her decline
among oils & lotions
seeing the first honest smile
of a lifetime

You are a decent
man gentle beyond imagination
I will do everything I can to justify
the trust you place in me

Frankly
I thought when I dropped that letter
that I was mad on the long razor

slide back to childhood
dreams will be the death of us all
& had dignity permitted
I would have entered the chute
bellbottoms up & flapping
to retrieve it

It would embarrass
us all for you to know how moved
I am that you are coming here/

& since I seem intent
on speaking to you both
& despise deception especially
my own let me begin again formally

Dear Bill & Sweet Kathleen my children
of light   I am nothing if not formal
Permit me the crudity of addressing
you both in one letter
The truth is

The only excuse for beginning anything
again is in those words the truth is
the admission that all that has gone before
is a lie & the hope beyond all reason
that what follows will not be

The truth is
I have been defeated repeat defeated
for the ten thousandth time at prose
I had the innocence to try once more
to write the great American something
or other & no doubt will again I'm sure

when I know beyond even small quarrel
that I have not one whit the character
necessary for anything
but short poems very short

You Billy
will write the great American something
or other but I have read nothing
& never will & will end badly
adrift without friends
better than I will deserve

My last sentence torn
from the carriage in a yellow crumple
lying portside now reads

Sweetness
& light left Mudville about this time
we on its heels   Closer to the sea . . .

Isn't that just dot dot dot
My but aren't I just
dot dot dot

My brain unravels
in prose sentence by sentence
five pages & I'm hanging on the screen
with the lizards
I want desperately
my magnum opus my periplum something
Homeric & grand want nothing else
frankly

I was born the wrong man
in the wrong time . . .

. . . .

Barbara Bradford do you know her
Taught English to illiterate freshmen
like myself when I was there & maybe
still does Well there is really
no civilized way to handle this
so what the hell here it is

We had a love affair
Barbara & I & since
I was her student &
it was most indiscreet
we let not a soul know

Even now you must not
that covey of old maid professors
would land on her jackals & magpies
promise me

                    So bring me word of her
will you I dare not write to her
for I am in love with her still
I write poems to her will
for the rest of my life

                              Isn't this
the silliest goddamn thing
you have ever heard

                              Go see her
for me & hold her hand ask her
about her health or the weather
or her brother

                         What is it
that all the women I love

have brothers they buy
sports cars for

                    Someone
told me she was Dean of Women
at some fancy eastern girls school
but I refuse to believe it//

Persuade your blushing bride Billy
not to use so many exclamation
points
        or I will fall
upon her in a fever

Don't tell me I was young
once myself it is not
true

    l&k paul

* * *

Kathleen Kathleen as I live
& breathe my death you are
sweet you are the one I love
you & hardly know you

The first thing I will tell
your genius husband on deplaning
is to watch you with Latin cunning
for I will find you in secret
at the first chance

                        What all
your funny questions amount to
is this

Can you live here
the way Mommy taught you

& the answer is absolutely not

There is no place like home
& no one like Mommy thank God
if you want the Brown Hotel in Louisville
then please go to the Brown Hotel
in Louisville

Come here
some other time
if you wish

There are lizards & bugs here
dirty children incurable disease
death nothing heroic that is not
essentially sad

Still
I fully expect you to depart
in finer health than you arrive
& forget about books I won't
let you read one
if you bring it

Is it not
enough to talk fish & drink
rum

I have a deep hatred
of books with which I will
infect you I am sure
& tourists
If you wear a funny hat & bring

a camera I will likely hit you
in the groin

                              Do women have groins

I talk to you this way because I love
you you myopic hussy
                                                  What gall
not to remember me I spoke to you
four or five times

                                          & I can be
depended upon to do any & everything
for those I love get you
bottles of aspirin
& mosquito spray

                                          Please
please it is all cared for food
lodging everything I have even
had the water of San Juan purified
just bring a pretty summer dress
& a bathing suit

                                      Your lodging
consists of two rooms one for privacy
part of the house the other
like my room screened on the open roof
a vent pipe standing guard
            As I write these words
I can see us at the table there
two roofs over
                                  You can expect
a flower color of your choice
standing in the vase on your arrival

             You can I
promise turn right around

& go back if you become ill
or unhappy   Nothing
is inexorable no
big steps only
many small ones
No grand passions
only many sweet loves

Ah well
you are a sweet & tender young
thing of my own description
something I have never been
How am I to know what goes
through such a head

I am
used to the islands & the islanders
trust me I will hover about you
with smiles & the latest issue
of the New Yorker generally
protect you from the foggy dew

If you were my own fair bride
I would not be so solicitous
It is my belief that a woman
if she is to be lived with
must be totally disillusioned
then rebuilt with care
An idea
which has proved unworkable
to date

Don't be dull & don't
believe anything you hear
about any place or anybody
even if I say it

Yr Servant paul

* * *

I had every hope of getting out
of this alive but the truth is
no such thing is possible ever
The truth is I am almost afraid
to say anything We have all
had such good response
one to the other It is all
very good & new very exciting

The truth is I have avoided as usual
saying the one thing this letter was
meant to say

                Instead I spoke as usual
of my defeat as though it were not
inevitable & beside the point
Laid it I see now portside
at your feet Praeder
in a yellow crumple
such a pity

                Fuck the defeats
the truth is I am again suffering
them   The truth is I am again
writing   The truth is I cannot
tell you what your letters
mean to me
& this visit

Perhaps we are
even honest perhaps
we can purify one
another holding
our distant mirrors

up to nature &
to ourselves
I believe it

//These poems
then what does one say I began
this letter with little else in mind
some civilized way to put them
into your hands
& tried to end it
without even sending them
What does one say indeed
You are the first to see them
not even Barbara

I could not
tolerate some horsesass
at the Antioch Review
defining himself
in their presence

I do hope
you will bring word of Barbara
it weighs into the silence at the end
of each sentence heavy among all things
I say & cannot say I will not mention
it again cannot you must understand
It is of course no matter

They look meager enough
a few dozen lines

thirty two years
going on sixty

I find it impossible to talk
about them to think
about them even

                I go off
in small motions
of dread
turning back
on myself
embarrassed & hurt

The one called Light
is simply the typographic
expression of dragonflies
mating over a black lake quite
beautiful

                The only hitch is
the female eats the male
for supper after love

First I called it Light
then Song #8 for Barbara
then Light again

Which I suppose come to think
of it is the story of my life

Too bad

Love to you both   paul

. . . .

4.22.56 / Calle Sol SJPR

Well as I live & breathe
you are the one both
my Billy my Lotus

            I spin in the air
above your heads light
& cunning
               Hellow there
hellow there indeed
now listen Billy

you have written a good poem
yet another as usual I am
rolled over on my back feet
in the air with admiration

But you are too smart for your own
good I am sure of it   Do you know
what I mean

                  In Washington there is
a museum which is better than most
not I think because of the paintings
they hold but because of the man
who hangs them   You must go there
immediately if possible this very day
for they have finally shown El Greco
for the fraud he is

                        A man of no true
feeling of large & suave gesture
theatrical in the worst sense broad

& unclean & facile
& worse
an evil man for he purports
to be religious Toledo
& saints & light aspiring
faces to the blue heavens
God in the backstays of the sun
topaz cloudfists
I hate the man
intensely

If I ever have children
I will permit them to play in the street
& talk to strangers & pick mushrooms
but never to look at El Greco without me
present

& so in Washington
some curator all he did
was hang him next to Goya

& that is that

No arrows no critics
in the wings no whispers

But there it all is
Next to Goya the man
is undone
revealed
You want
to make holes
in the canvas
hang him
in tar

You are not El Greco surely
if delivering newspapers has done nothing
else it has kept you modest

any more
I suspect than you could become Goya
or would want to for that matter

But five lines often are enough
if you pay for them n'est-ce pas
You carry around too many words
in your mouth Billy
& they come out too easily
you are brighter than you are deep
in this poem which is not you
Ask uncle Paul the smartest
man alive

You ain't
holy & surely I ain't
holy
but good poetry can be

Throw the impostors out all the old turds
& never write a poem
you don't absolutely
have to

And drink
at least one glass
of milk every day

. . . .

It is I fear
a long life
to be dealt with
day by day eyes

close in look not
back or to the future
be still neat
in small hopes

Already I can see my last
years friendless &
wandering
                I refuse to believe it

But the equal truth is
my dear Bill & Kathleen
& I will not darken it further

Your letter brought me back
from the dead

I cannot believe
you are coming

I have looked on it
with such odd extravagance someone
to talk to
to walk with

I have too much time to think
& not heart enough
to sustain myself

. . . .

from

section TWO

of

Praeder's Letters

5:05 AM
6.13.56 / SJPR

Bill

I will slide this under your door
on my way to the base   If Kathleen intercepts it
that is no great matter   It will save me the trouble
of writing to her separately
which I can't attempt until
late tonight

                    I trust
that it was clear to all parties
on the steps a couple of hours ago
that our plans for dinner together
tonight are canceled

                                        A big mistake
has been made I fear many little ones
will get dumped in on top of it every time now
we get together   Clarity on this
is of utmost importance to me to all of us
though I speak only for myself of course
and hope that you and your bride
will do likewise

                              A hangover
actually helps otherwise
I might act as I too
often have   To please

We take off our sweaty blouses in SJ
we push the piano away from the wall
we shoot craps we stay up all night

the CG is full of questionable people
the islands full of questionable places
We end up dancing drunk too often
saying and doing things inadmissable
come daylight
                    Forgetfulness
may be man's sole virtue
Forget it Billy
Okay

I don't blame you caro
If I had your bride for my own
I would be worse company than you
if such is imaginable   She asks a lot
your young lady & it's not as apparent
as she seems to think what right she has
to ask for more than a little
her distress notwithstanding
Bossiness knows only itself
& can't learn   Coupled with youth
it's ugly company & exhausting
A leading-role mentality
needs a good script

She has attributes
but self-knowledge
isn't among them
I feel for you

                  Look last night
could happen again I wouldn't promise
that it won't even if I could   Fear
is one thing worry another   Worry
is an ass wart hermano
painfully located
I'm not your baby sitter
I'm not your bride's baby sitter

Nor am I the messenger of your fitful union
once this note is finished

Your fitful union
distressed me at first now it bores me
The idea of three more weeks of it
takes hold of me first in the sphincter
& that's the easy part

Our situation
terrifies me frankly it exhausts me

You should have gone on back to your place
Billy my boy   You were a thankless piece of work
hovering around the door generally
being put upon
You have a talent for it
the power of one who truly believes
in being wronged

Have you considered going back to Lexington
with or without your bride
I think you should
Consider it I mean
Don't tell me it's impossible
The list of impossibilities
is too long already

If you're worried about Kathleen
and what she'll do
you ought to be
I am
She is

A child is a lot to get used to
I'm sure of it
it may be impossible
but leave me out of it

okay   I'm providing her
with similiar instructions

She says that she wants you to leave her alone period
that she has tried on numerous occasions to communicate
this to you and that you refuse to understand
She says that she'll take up speaking with you
again when she sees fit

I promised her like the fool I am
that I would relay this message

I don't want to hear your side of the story
I didn't want to hear hers
I never will
It's just the kind of guy I am

We'll get through this
If you need money
I've got money

I'll feel something for you again
& maybe even you for me
I'm not counting on it though
I'm counting on you Billy

p

* * *

Irritation and impatience aren't feelings
they're spleen blocking the heart
You are too young to be this far from home
& it's all my fault
                              I'm sorry

Everything I say to you
is what I refuse to know
about myself
                    & I don't have the excuse of youth

. . . .

from

section THREE

of

Praeder's Letters

9.26.56/SJPR

. . . .

Advice
is useless projection malo
moonshine in the dirt never
take it especially from me
So here
is my advice   Why don't you get
out of Lexington

Tell me I know
not what I say & it is true
but the truth is
the truth is
. . .

I'll stop
that is the only decent
thing to do & I am nothing
if not decent nothing
indeed

The final truth is
there is no disorder
but it takes a saint
nothing less
The waves
have mercy the rocks no
mercy at all
You're the waves
Billy as you always have been
Suck it up is what waves do

I would send you
my hawkbell mi poeta had it
sufficient character

amor   p

. . . .

10.17.56/SJPR

Dear Bill/

Things go badly
with me
I have nothing
to share
& love
no one

This is why
you & I
quarreled here

I am empty

not shallow
but empty

And so will you be
in a few years

I heard about
you & Kathleen
sorry

Get an older chick
next time

                    Few women
understand anything
but the more age
they acquire the more

they learn to look
sweet wise & helpful
quietly

Maybe your heart
is broken
if so I am
sorry

love & kisses P

. . . .

11.7.56 SJPR

. . . .

The truth is your letter
it has moved me deeply
You are suffering
I am sorry
                But
there is no way
around it
        not if you want to be
a man & not if you want
to write poetry

                    Writing
is no answer but when you feel
deeply there is little else to do

What you say now
is of no importance
A real affection
is rising
in you

          There are men
around me daily who have at life
& have at women & they
are nothing

                It is the quality
of the affection that matters
the only thing
You know that
better than I

Tragedy/Women
Love/Children

Fuck them all
Billy
        Leave them to men
whose eyes have not been torn
out of their heads
by what they have seen

                                        You may not
believe this you may not be ready
to believe this yet/still
in your suffering you
have made yourself responsible
to the empty air
to God
to the world
it is all the same

Men & women
may love you
but you cannot
love them
no matter
how you try
& it will
in time
kill you

            All that you
can have & it is
by no means certain
that you will attain it
is greatness a great
spirit
        & agony will
in time have no meaning

The poet is the proud snail Billy
We watch him for the whaleroads
he makes on stone & concrete

The waving stalks
of his eyes
in the early light
The rhythmic contractions
of his slimy sidelit body
The colorful wakes
of his secretions

. . . .

9.2.57/ D.C.

. . . .

I told her [Barbara Bradford]
of my literary successes
& she cried

I don't know
how to explain this
or anything else
I don't understand
anything that happens
especially between men
& women

She did marry a reverend
it lasted not a month
was annulled
I asked no questions
there are no answers
anyway

I was delighted
& relieved to see
her   Can you believe it
I am sure you can

//I've been having an affair
with a woman from Cleveland
doesn't that sound shitty
I moved into a new apartment
last week to escape her but
it didn't work nothing ever does
She was here in fact when your letter
arrived breaking my back
with protestations & prostrations
She wants to move in with her guitar
& potter's wheel   Every man does

the best he can   She has me nailed
to the floor the ceiling I feel
like a Godless Chagall
in glossy black & white

Your comments about love
made me sigh

                    The grand passion
is not for me really
or anyone else
                    To hold
hands & be quiet is
enough
          When the passion
is grand it is not
the woman you love
it's yourself

               /Listen
if I cannot go to France
October next I will try
to visit you in SFran okay
Have you wowed them I dare say
What is there in the lit life
beside Howl & how is westcoast
pussy
       Forgive me I seem intent
on being a fool this morning

. . . .

from

section FOUR

of

Praeder's Letters

10.5.57/ D.C.

Dear Bill

            I cannot tell
what time is the right time
or which words carry best

The fact is Kathleen and I
were married a few days ago

Somehow we both expected this
in a strange and unsaid way

Very well   It is a fact
I ask your indulgence

No one knows of this yet
just the immediate immediates
We will live in Washington

More than this is perhaps
only talk
            for small mouths
small hours

                Between men
in matters of moment etc
I believe simplicity
is desirable

                I could
scarcely say I am not
anxious to hear
your comment

Perhaps you are
the only person
I will ask
for an opinion

Very well again very well

If I sound dreadfully final
about all this it is because
having reached deep now into
my thirty-third year I
am not lightly committed
to this marriage
and being so accustomed
to light commission
I stand in danger
of taking too much
grim determination
into it

          I wish merely
to live with Kathleen
and of course the young man
and to try for the stability
I have so far not achieved

Yes certainly
I am too grim

                    //I should shut up
now & send this I know that
& you know I know it but
it's like everything else
I know useless

. . . .

10.21.57 /WASHINGTON

. . . .

A life time
is very bloody long
and a week or so
doesn't matter to me
one way or the other //

What do you think
of my eventual adoption
of your son

I do think
it probably best
for the young man
especially when he starts school etc

Let me know
how you feel
about this
and if all is
agreeable
I will proceed
with the necessary
papers etc

Lawyers
doctors generals
the professionals
of this world
strike terror
in me

O by the way
Kathleen withdrew from Indiana

and from the academy in general
for at least the next few years
I am very pleased at this

Love Paul

* * *

Let me hear something
I think of you more often
than you might imagine

. . . .

3.3.60/ NYC

Dear Bill

Forgive me
this scrawl but
I've put this off
too long already

About the young man
can we wait

I am in mid-
air suspended
the dark
vast & middle

I'm worse company than usual

The time is not right
there is too much
that is new
adjustments
must be made
more time
is needed

I think we all need more
time

Kathleen is young
& easily frightened
I swore that I would never
again live in NYC

There are times
when I understand everything
times when I understand nothing

//The Avenue is not as bad
as I imagined   I meet
serious people daily
I hope before long
to get back to my own
writing
            Though I am
past the point
where I think
it matters

                Kathleen
and the young man
are well

            The baby is
recovering from a cold
her first of the season

Thank you for your
thoughtfulness //

                        Each year
I think that if I can just
get through the winter
sanity will return
but of course
it never does

love & kisses paul

. . . .

9.28.67/NYC

Dear Bill

                    I am sorry
about all this but
it was unavoidable
I took a job in Atlanta
Kathleen did not
want to move again
and certainly one could not
blame her but
I was ready to kill
my boss
                Now
we're back in NYC & I'm back
at Thompson   They fired
the little piece of shit
If I believed in triumphs
I would take this to be one

                              I have never
been more or less than I am
irritable selfish pained
at what I see and cannot
see in time   I speak
more often than not
in a passion
We all know that

The doctor assures us
the stuttering is nothing
to get upset about
But do you know that I see
you
every morning
at my breakfast
you

put your finger
in my coffee
& eat my cigarettes
you
untie my shoes
you
come out
of the door
as I go in
I shout at you
& receive for answer
the ultimate look eyes
quiet not scornful
He is so much like
you
& the thing is
like you
quiet gentle complex
enigmatic
It is enough to drive me
insane
But since I am insane
already & accept
the extranatural
then okay okay
I should adopt him
I should have adopted him
years ago but
still I cannot
I try to be good
to him
worrisome & protective
but we are all strange
to one another still
still

Things are difficult
to keep end to end
I do what I can

we all do what we can
& it is not good enough
by many times over

I do not think practically
I should adopt him
until we settle down
to one another/

The new child
is a new child
what more can one say

I will come to love her
I am sure as I have the first
but all I can see now
is that she has nothing
between her legs
nothing

Love Paul

* * *

Listen the boy is fine please
don't worry   He wants to be
a ballplayer like you
                                        I must go
& barbecue can you believe it
I am sure you can

4.14.69 / Mt. Kisco

. . . .

I think
of the millions sitting there
in the blue light night
after night the sweet
flypaper of their empty eyes
their empty lives
hanging there
in the blue light
waiting to be had
& I choose my images
with care

Yr fateful servant Praeder

* * *

Listen
about your novel I am
glad you brought it up
but let's drop it okay
It was your story too
& still is & still is
& anyway it was a long time ago
& in another country
& anyway the wench
is dead
Who you
sent copies to
is your business

I won't say
I did not hate
you at the time
because I did

Don't forget who taught you
what poetry is Billy

Love Paul

NEW POEMS

Belly Ring Elegies

At the Urinal

Okay gottcha I know
what you have in your hand
I know what you're doing
How many times today
will you be so sure
where you are
what you're up to
How many times today
will you be so relieved
and unquestioning
Think about it
No one else today
will be so grateful to you
as you are to yourself
your bladder emptying
your satisfaction real ahh
At least this once
you turn away
with clarity
concerning your behavior
with the way you've spent your time

A Poem

A poem is a stage
not a conduit

Eight words so far
I need more

I open a book
bang I have a word

Then more than one
With my eyes closed bango

ha words come to me
as long as I don't care which ones

They jump up on me with their
whispers their right to be called lordship

Throw some words at it
a poem says why not

Some might stick
Briefly

SOME OF THIS SMOKE NEEDS MOVING

What else is a guy supposed to think
for a goodly number of long minutes
he reckons hey that was that
there is no further act
Even the tumbleweed stays put
in her dusty backroom mirror
smokes stands still
in her lopsided boots
Her long limbs spent
sleep a sleep
of nakedness

                    A few tailgates
the lady has lifted & hooked
                                        yes she has &
pulled up a few guy wires oh
the wind now singers
may call it Mariah
leggy trouble up there
where she works
but tower workers
we call it howling

                    Hey
your gentleman's back
to renew you Mariah
hey with his own leg-
songs for a cowgirl
once clothed & with his long forefinger
tracing where the lucky levis get to seam
Your eyes could open now but don't
That's cute yes it is
You can smile now
whenever you're ready

we know you
When you come back freshened
he'll want to see what you're wearing
Mariah when you walk out of the walk-in closet
                                                                                Oh hurry
just a little after opening & closing so many drawers

Please

Three quarters & a dimple
that's my way of describing
your spirit manifest
in your face
and in the intonations of your voice
and the attitudes therein
Your voice withholds
the results
favors the process
When your hands get up
around your face
hey

For Mary Ann

    I'll ring you up
I'll say dearest
You'll answer
with that laugh

Don't quit laughing
There'd be no counting the people
jerked headlong into grief

Here's the boogie deal
I keep ringing you up
You keep picking up the call

A While Back

A while back
I tied a silky red bow
around each thing hereabouts
The middle toe of her right foot
The walkabout gray phone
The black plastic bag
of garbage even
the catalogs
(all except one
I won't embarrass her by saying which)

It was then that she awoke
It was morning it was then
that she brushed her teeth
and did one following another
her other things

                    Later
            how much later
I'm not sure
            empty shoes
toed to the wall at an angle
provided one clue among many

Oh shoes empty but not bereft
take me to her again
and again she was here
a while back
I'm sure of it

The Lady's Name

What had seemed important at the time
was replaced by what hadn't been noticed
The way the century rode the handrail up
as rings of light on her left hand
Here she cometh
                                        A figure
of your erotic life
You're free now
As you see fit
Once upon a time

the lady dropped a lavender favorite
to her bedside floor for you
to see & never forget

You want to know the details
of the noise she makes
& when she makes it
& how it makes
those who hear it feel

        Not the clogs back & forth yadda
yadda on the hardwood
give us a break
Her love song
detail upon detail

You peer out a peephole
when she comes & goes
Dare you call her by name

Go ahead
                    The lady
will answer Answer
is the lady's name

A l'Ombre des Jeunes Filles en Fleurs

I can't believe she says this
She says *I'm in the caution mode*
I tell her I can't believe she said that
Caution mode now really oh wow
Let me write this down

There's too much any more I can't believe
She knows this and takes advantage of me
All I want is to detail her like always

If you get a live person any more at the end
of the line you laugh and celebrate until
the live person at the other end laughs
& celebrates with you
                              That's what
was happening when she got cautious

Maybe her cell phone rang and I didn't hear
I have a 12thC mind

Where she's sitting and how she's sitting
there and what all surrounds
our picnic I'm not
going to tell you
it's so unporno

If it's a mode I'm not in it
The minute it gets to be a mode
I'm out
        That's just the kind of guy
I am
          reaching into her shadow
& slapping her thigh

Starting there
Now I've got her attention
She of the caution mode

What's a caution mode
ever done for you I want to know
I don't say this rather it's a look I have

If she wasn't dealing
at fox she is now
El fox
puts his touch
behind her

Who wouldn't be cautious
out here in a public park
strangers paying attention
in the keep of a poet
whose honor
is in audacity

Please
this prisoner of embarrassment
says to her shameless consort
Please please don't you dare
adding to his excitement
as maybe now she means to

There's this one in particular it's hers
Loose tongue whispers details into her ear
A blanket Woodland Park end of the century

*

No one has to tell me that
hard-ons aren't a way of life
But dealing with them is

I'll speak again
if I have something
further to report

The Approaching Sky

Fresh Snow at Dusk

The solitary light of the ridge barn
in response to time
gets steadily brighter
The world its giant eyes
growing accustomed
to the dark
turns deep
purple
cow shapes
the darkest
A day
that had never been departs
of its own colors
Along the ridge the slow shapes
of the herd change
as they come in to feed
A calf left behind
at some cold turn bawls
A cow stops in profile then another
their long-throated bellowing turned backwards
& etched
Fresh cold
in the last light
& snow

TIME

Here
Here
Here
Need I say more
How can I
Who could
              It will be left
there in time

Spring

I was all up in the eyes
when the sun fell upon me
shutting me down in the pupils
Light and dark became my sudden work
I'd been there before
among the names
of several things
I took the closest
new firepole of air
and spun downwards
When I reached stability
again the crocuses
had arrived
Were moving
Some one color
Others another

Poet

He sleeps
upside down
like a cave bat
& knows
the world
through his ear
large & convoluted
each thing by its echo
He flits about
in your eyesight
like floaters
like anything
up from the depths
into the mirror

Fire

I didn't know whose hands were whose
especially the one reaching
                                          You
saw it did you know
which fast shadows to trust flying
up the wall into the corners
                                           Bats
came loose on whose skin
was it
       You felt it how
unlikely it all was fire
flying them holy
with silent acts

We waited for sounds that never came
from those who could not be
otherwise or elsewhere
We heard ourselves

When it was dark again when
what the fire reached for
turned out to be
what it touched
I thought well
why not
            We
have features
sweet seed
Tell me one thing
then another
          Touch
the whole deal
in a slow pivot
Keep thine eyes shut
the small of thy back
in my hand's tow

Rothko

Early on there was a mother alone
with one or two children a girl
and a small boy from Russia
The figures remained
Their shapes changed

In dim light he sat alone in the middle
he crossed his legs he smoked

Great lungs of color breathed him
into a dissolution of history
He descended there was no
bottom and the buoyancy
there held his breath
breathed him out
The colors multiplied
Each pulsed around its
vanishing point

In time they muted

Occasionally he would move two
of the large somber canvases closer
together by a few inches
he would lift one a little farther
off the floor
Oh the gods

He came from far off
to live in his eyes

in the dim light
and vast middle

He was big He sweated He was angry
A portrait painter who wanted to be clear
and understood though not transparent

Two empty paint-splattered shoes
on the orange sleeping bag in the middle
of a gray studio floor
his sock feet
one foot after another
going deliberately up
the creaking stairs

His shapes were actors
Their first role color

In the next act they came to him
and they hovered in stacks
of two three four
They bowed inward

In the last act
they hoped the hope
that comes of light
They acted without shame

Mouse Elegy

Within the weathered barn
this drama of back-lit cat walking along
the dusty crossbeam so cat-likely stepping
over tobacco sticks
The step ladder
by which he got up there
leaning against its shadow
in the tack room
two western saddles
on saw horses one english several bridles
hanging from large nails the smell of old leather
and wintergreen
All this
and the countless rest
in the tack room alone countless
goes down whether or not we show up
of a Tuesday to smell and to be grateful

and to hear the scream and
the after-scream
In the late August afternoon
dusty Kentucky light
stirred up

Following the scuffle
the next sound
had duration

but no name
        A parenthesis opened
and closed
    with nothing inside

Next the skull being eaten

Followed in due course
by one horse whinnying
                              Later
another kicking the stall

Then a whoosh of starlings
leaving a nearby tree

Ridge Owl Black Dog

Willie is old his face white
the white crawls up his forehead
and over his ears nowadays whenever
he lifts his tired white face up off
the floor it's to say
this may be the last time
you guys show a little feeling
I say do you want to go out
directing the question to the white
on white surrounding his eyes
like an owl's
                At the sound
of the O word Willie's
old nozzle hits the floor
his head retreats into his shoulders
his imploring eyes feature cataracts
and self-pity
                        It's painful for him
to stand any more more an adventure
than he wants to undertake getting over the sill
and down the one flagstone step
                                        a large
plain yellow dog mostly lab a field creature
the main dog for years headlong through tall grass
through thickets fearless with the neighboring pitbull
Nowdays he moves only to stay close indoors only
occasionally does his bark sound familiar
When the owl of the ridge woods gets going
The rest of the time he's deaf
His nails stiff-legging it along behind
you over the hardwood at feed time
can break your heart
                    Last night
in the middle of the night I
heard them in a dream in the dream they
were clicking in circles around

the hollow house trying
to remember something themselves
to begin with maybe the owl
maybe a way back to Mary Ann
An echoing
                The sound
of his heavy hobbling nails
on hardwood slipping
every few steps was the same
in the dream as in waking life
except the hobble had nothing to follow was wandering
from room to hollow room and then back
No master no friends
No owl of the ridge
Not even a trace

Jake the monster black dog
who's come to live here
despite everything we can do
lies curled up in the leaves
or under a bush out one door or another
sometimes on Willie's backporch cushion

We don't feed the monster
We don't make over him
We treat Jake like he's not here

Still the owl up on the ridge there
won't get going won't even check in
Maybe the owl on the ridge up there
isn't up there any longer
that's what the dream
seems to me to be about
how Jake's presence changes everything
Where the cats will agree to be fed
Whether we can lure Willie
out the door for his business
I tell myself to wake up
I say Willie needs you

He's lost he's lost it
But I stay asleep until
the sound of his loose bowels hits
the floor and wall in the front room

Thick shitty blood that's what I think
he's slipped and fallen into thrashing about
in the half-light from the hallway
                                                            I think
the seizure tracking him for months
has finally caught up and grabbed him
                                                                        My hand
to his quivering head helps him hold on
                                                                  Mary Ann
I cry out

                    Together we quiet him and clean him up
as best we can inside the house the floor and walls
as best we can at night
                                        Come morning
we hose him down out back and towel him

which entails facing the nemesis Jake
who gets one long whiff of Willie's quiver
and at nightfall disappears that's exactly
what he did

            Where is the big black dog
who's not coiled up in the leaves
or under a dark bush with Willie
asleep at my feet again
And the ridge owl back
with its O sounds egg-
like alliterations deep-
throated and feathery

Is he off getting fed
Is he on his way back

Name Age Country Next of Kin

The soldiers kneel over the wounded child cold
after rain
        Wired to her wrist a large tag
One has his hand behind her long scrawny neck
Her mouth is open
We are waiting
to see if she can
take water

The Wars

They hang around in some grand image
Achilles storming back & forth in the dust
Mongolian hordes on tail-flying horseback
The stacks of the dead at Antietam
sorted out by uniform color
Paratroopers night-dropped
behind Nazi lines
the weather freezing
Even the Fall itself
from one into two & on
into many lying awake
back to back
their eyes open
in the tent dark

& through the center
of the human dream
at a dead run
four of us
with strong hands carry
a fifth in an improv sling
                    His boots stick out
swollen with dried mud
                              Witnessed in newsprint
by his mother his children & their countrymen
as their leader talks & talks

The Approaching Sky

I told the story of a child
in a big place of wandering
from window to tall window
fearful of the approaching sky
and then forgot I ever
told it until I heard
the story again today
on the news
                    There
were two of them Boys
A settlement the Israelis
called it Spring 2001 Both
in the joy of their bodies
thirteen and fourteen playing
hooky in a nearby power place
known for its caves

The younger bolder
by nature got closer

Once his eyes adjusted
what did he see inside
looking back at him
How many were there

Or did they come up behind
heard before seen
How many were there
picking up stones

Imagine a conversation
There may have been one

Can I stop now
Isn't this enough

Who wants to see what happened

next which Arab wielded
how many stones
in what fashion
                    As he had had
done unto him no beginning
                                To see the skulls broken
and bleeding at the cave entrance and witness
the exultation of children hand-painting in blood
the walls and the exaltation of the elders
before these new cave paintings
                                        Get back get back get back

you leaders in Tel Aviv Jerusalem Ramala
History is upon you as it always
has been Your children
are in the bargain and now mine

What would we teach them
in thought and in deed
beyond our hatreds

Our tactics and strategies
Our sense of history our pride
        What is it we're proud of
Is it love or something less
than love
        Has our power
driven us crazy so crazy
we don't know what crazy
is any longer
            Or is it our pride
Or is it our money
Can it be our money

Who wants to know
what our money has done to us
what we have done to others
under its spell

Let's teach our children
to pray why not
we could use the challenge
In the presence of eternity
how do we present ourselves
Do we pray in thoughts
or in deed only
off camera
the rest bullshit
Is it easy to pray
I was taught that it's easy
to pray but not taught what prayer is
Loss taught me that
And then again

Here's one of its lessons
Pray to yourself only and often
Pray for love in your heart
Enough for your thoughts to clarify

Here's what we have to look at
The floors give way within the towers
White dust settles over the city
Wandering loss holds its pictures up
begging for us to look please please look
Has anyone seen the loved ones

I'm only a guy another guy
off here in the boondocks
thousands of miles away
How can anyone formulate
the challenge
                    Oh
we leaders
Some day
one of us
or more

will put an end
to this madness
Clear the way
for the next
Is that what we have to offer
Love forgotten ignored lost

For Matthew Shepard & His Mother

Let me answer the phone first
have the joyless lunch with the guy
write the letter no one will read
worry again about money argue again
in my hurt head with him or her

When enough is enough
at the end of every century
& at the beginning of the next
at the end of every year &
at the beginning of the next
& so on month day hour

Whose child this time
Whose mother or father

The white glove lying palm up
on the margin of the trail
fingers cut off at the first knuckle

A watertank somewhere in the picture

Let me shed two things for every one
I pick up along the way to three
four & so on
until I am naked
before the fence post
where Matthew Shepard was
tortured & crucified
by sexual hatred

The markings scattered
the snow lifting the muddy ruts
until past midnight
At dawn
down the hill the sound

of a weakening car battery
A love song faint
then not so faint
through the open window
of the passing pickup
Then faint again

Only when I look into the boy's closed eyes
will his mother look back
from before her mother was born
her right eye her right eye
my right eye my right eye
All the way back
to fire & water

Some day I will die
my children will die
maybe even before me
Oh I couldn't stand that
anything but that please

Every day I'm not called
to the morgue for identification
I make a list of my blessings
as many as I can remember
I bow repeatedly
not once without pain

I chant the names & exploits of Trip & Burr
of Matthew & Michael & Larry
I chant Mary Ann & Annie Annie
until the chant begins to chant
Oh Lisa & Melissa & Rebecca oh Julia
& Arwen & Robert & Daniel & Maya
Oh Whitney & Sarah Wylie & Angela

And as for the eyes looking back
Well there they are

Title Index

Because the selections from *Praeder's Letters* do not have conventional titles, they are listed only in the index of first lines.

Index of First Lines

Former Poet Laureate of Kentucky, **James Baker Hall** is a widely sought-after ambassador of the state's exceptional literary culture. Winner of a Stegner Fellowship in fiction at Stanford, an NEA fellowship in poetry writing, a Southern Arts Fellowship in photography, and the prestigious Pushcart and O. Henry prizes, he is an artist of extraordinary talent and accomplishment. The *New Yorker, Poetry*, the *Paris Review*, the *Hudson Review*, the *Sewanee Review*, and the *Kenyon Review* are among the many magazines to publish his poems. He has taught at Stanford, NYU, MIT, and the University of Connecticut. From 1973 to 2003 he was a professor of creative writing at the University of Kentucky.
(Photograph by Rebecca Howell)